APR 2008

ED

HOW TO SLAY

INSPIRATION FROM THE QUEENS & KINGS OF BLACK STYLE

HOW TO SLAY

INSPIRATION FROM THE QUEENS & KINGS OF BLACK STYLE

CONSTANCE C. R. WHITE

Rizzoli
NEW YORK

New York · Paris · London · Milan

CONTENTS

8   FOREWORD BY VALERIE STEELE

10   INTRODUCTION

18   ORIGINAL DIVAS

38   LAID

62   EBONICS

78   AFRO-CHIC

102 BARE BEAUTIES

116 NATURAL HAIR & OTHER CROWNS

146 COUPLES

158 SASHAY, SHANTÉ

174 MANOLOGY

204 AMERICAN CLASSICS

220 ACKNOWLEDGMENTS

223 PHOTO CREDITS

For Denrick, Nefatari, Kimathi,

Nkosi, Keith, Chressmore, Alison, and Randy,

I am grateful to have you in my life.

This book is dedicated to my dear friend

Margo, a lover of people, a lover of luxury,

a woman of great style and vision.

FOREWORD

African Americans have had a major impact on fashion over the past century. Yet their style and influence has still not been fully acknowledged. Constance White's book makes an important contribution to popular awareness of the significance of style in the Black community—and its impact on fashion culture worldwide.

Already in the 1920s, Harlem was a veritable fashion parade. Photographs taken in America's greatest Black metropolis document an explosion of style. In part, this represented a new prosperity within segments of the Black community. But equally, it was the result of a new sense of hopefulness, epitomized by the Harlem Renaissance. Confronted with flagrant racism in other parts of America, in Harlem Black flappers and dandies felt free to dress in fashionable fur coats alongside new automobiles. Participation in the First World War also alerted African Americans to new possibilities in Europe, and many decamped to Paris, where Josephine Baker, in particular, became a style icon.

To dress fashionably had long been a point of pride for African Americans. Photographs of Frederick Douglass in the 1800s, for example, always show him dressed formally, as a gentleman. African Americans have also participated in the fashion system as tailors, dressmakers, milliners, and retailers. Anne Cole Lowe created beautiful custom-made gowns for leaders of society. Most famously, Lowe made Jaqueline Kennedy's wedding dress. In Paris, designers such as Yves Saint Laurent employed many Black models, but in the United States, for many years, the catwalk was almost entirely segregated. The Ebony Fashion Fair, founded and directed by Eunice Johnson, provided a rare venue for Black fashion models.

In the late 1950s and 1960s, the civil rights movement in the United States, like the anti-colonial movement in Africa and Asia, brought an awareness of the political aspects of appearance. It was no longer enough to look "respectable." Black men and women embraced the idea that "Black is beautiful," rejecting Eurocentric beauty standards, epitomized by the process of hair straightening. Black pride was symbolized by hairstyles like the Afro and Afrocentric dress embracing a host of garments and textiles, most famously kente cloth. The Black Panther Party created a militant and glamorous look with leather coats, turtleneck shirts, sunglasses, and revolutionary berets.

From jazz to reggae, soul, rap and hip hop, the music of the African diaspora has transformed popular culture, including fashion culture. Jazzmen, like Miles Davis, pioneered cool styles, which influenced menswear around the world. The Rastafarian style of Bob Marley and other reggae icons continues to have staying power. From Nina Simone to Diana Ross, Black singers have inspired with voice and style. Rappers Run-D.M.C. made Adidas popular, and hip hop's gold chains eventually even invaded the runways of Chanel. The brilliance of Black athletes has also long been recognized, and, like performers, many athletes—from Muhammad Ali to Venus and Serena Williams—have been kings and queens of style.

Studies have demonstrated that creativity flourishes when diversity is present. Yet it was only in the 1970s that Black fashion designers, like Stephen Burrows, Patrick Kelly, Willi Smith, Jeffrey Banks, and Scott Barrie, began to be widely recognized. Although still underrepresented in the fashion industry, today there are more important Black fashion designers than ever before, including Tracy Reese, Sean John, Olivier Rousteing of Balmain, Grace Wales Bonner, Mimi Plange, and Shayne Oliver of Hood By Air. Similarly, Black fashion models, from Naomi Sims and Pat Cleveland to Iman, Veronica Webb, Alek Wek, and Naomi Campbell, have appeared on magazine covers and runways internationally.

Over the past decades, a multiplicity of Black styles has flourished, and Black style icons, such as Rihanna and Beyoncé, have been acclaimed around the world. But the Black Lives Matter movement has brought renewed attention to entrenched racism. When wearing a hoodie can result in the death of a young Black man, it is clear that style is political. In the present day, that principle finds its most vivid and inspiring incarnation in the elegance—in every sense of the word—of President and First Lady Barack and Michelle Obama.

Valerie Steele

INTRODUCTION

xploding down runways, in stores, online, and on Main Street—everywhere you look—style shaped by the African Diaspora is ubiquitous in fashion today for people of all colors, races, and creeds.

Some key factors drive its popularity, among them increased globalization, the Internet, and the desire of millennials of African descent to feel ownership of and know more about their African ancestry and history.

By now, multiculturalism may sound a bit banal, even cliché, but some of the old barriers have fallen like so many wooden matchsticks, and immigration moves apace. Today, we're as likely to see a Nigerian graduate student in her Holland-cloth peplum dress steering her Lexus down the streets of Houston as we are an African-American lawyer in Brooklyn rocking her box braids as she buys the latest hipster look from a high-low designer collaboration, such as Olivier Rousteing of Balmain for H&M. Rousteing is the first Black designer to head a major European label. He fits perfectly into the biracial, multicultural sweep of today's world. Along with British-Jamaican Grace Wales Bonner (winner of the 2016 LVMH Prize for Young Fashion Designers), Rousteing is one of a handful of young designers who reflect the hunger for Black style with their work and creative choices.

Like a rekindled love affair, this renaissance of Black style—dormant since the Black pride era of the Sixties and Seventies—embraces both familiar and new experiences. It feels as if we are experiencing a second coming of Black pride.

The fight-the-power Sixties and the decade that followed fomented calls for Black equality. Protestors took to the streets in clothes and hairstyles that became badges of the era, some crafted by those wearing them, and others created by designers. It became popular for Black people and some of the White people who stood with them to wear the uniform of pride and revolution: dashikis, African glass beads, the colors of Black liberation—red, green, and black—and black

OPPOSITE Curly-kinky hair has the capacity to coil upward, inspiring countless innovative styles like these plaited braids on actor-writer Nana Ghana.

leather jackets. Black style, in fact, has never completely disappeared; rather, its popularity ebbs and flows.

Surely today's blossoming Afrocentric fashion goes hand in hand with the robust Black Lives Matter movement against racial injustice. Does an internal awakening take place first, followed by the outward expression in the form of fashion and style? Or, conversely, do today's African Americans, particularly the youth, first adopt the style signifiers of cultural pride and awareness, which in turn awaken in them a need for racial justice and equality? When courageous NFL star Colin Kaepernick took a symbolic stand against police brutality by kneeling during the national anthem at the start of one of his games, something interesting happened. He put his curly-kinky hair in an Afro. Prior to that episode, Kaepernick was most often seen with his head shaved low or his hair in braids. Style can be superficial, but it can also undeniably be an expression of significant social, cultural, and economic realities. From Kaepernick's hair to Black women's decisions to perm their tresses—since at least as far back as the Sixties—decisions on these matters have been Faustian choices that affect employment and advancement in the workplace.

Fashion has embedded itself in our popular culture, and Black style, fertile and innovative, is continuously multiplying like a reproducing amoeba, spinning off into sub-genres comprising Afro-chic, Afro-punk, Afro-futurism, zoot, Afro-boho, Rasta, bobo dread, reality show style, sneaker head, church lady, sapes, Nigerian princess, dancehall queen, ghetto fabulous, rapper, Mother Africa, Fort Greene buppie, and Fruit of Islam.

These days, you cannot walk to Starbucks or attend a fashion event in New York, London, Milan, Paris—or Lagos, for that matter—without bumping into a street styler posing for a picture. As I dashed around the world taking in fashion shows, my matching London Fog luggage in tow (you thought I was going to say Louis Vuitton?), I saw so many innovative, effervescent expressions of Black street fashion. Fashion is more accessible than it's ever been. Touch your screen and Prada's Holland-cloth prints appear before you in their multihued glory. Touch again and you can order the roots version of that fabulous Prada frock in rich, authentic fabric from Zuvaa.com.

When Rihanna shimmered in New York at the Council of Fashion Designers of America awards in 2014 to accept a Fashion Icon Award, everyone there experienced shock and awe. Her sense of style—the risks she took—left a theater full of soigné designers and fashion editors, including the likes of Diane von Furstenberg, Michael Kors, and Anna Wintour, dumbfounded, a nearly impossible

OPPOSITE Beloved by chic millennials, the turban has re-emerged as an expression of Black pride, a hot accessory, and an easy way to protect fragile hair. This mash up of vintage African and Anglo patterns looks modern on Joy Adaeze, a blogger and entrepreneur.

feat. What hasn't this group seen? Maybe Rihanna in a dress that offered a lesson in anatomy. The singer took her sweet time mounting the steps to the stage to accept her award. In slow motion, every curve, every butt dimple was evident through her transparent glittery pink gown. The room went quiet. You could have shouted "fire" and no one would've moved.

I imagine that decades earlier another trailblazing, popular Black chanteuse, Josephine Baker, elicited similar stunned reactions from certain circles in Paris. You get that when you show up wearing nothing but a banana belt.

Music and fashion move together over time like two sinewy dancers playing off each other's rotating hips and sensuous footwork. Drummers from West Africa in their traditional djellabahs are iconic. Stateside and in parts of Europe in the early twentieth century, bandleaders like Cab Calloway popularized the dramatically baggy zoot suit. Jazzmen and blueswomen started trends, as Billie Holiday did when she appeared with a flower in her hair. The Twenties flapper style is said to have risen in part from the need to allow for vigorous movement after Black youth introduced an energetic new dance called the Charleston, which was then popularized on Broadway. With dresses shortened to scandalously bare ankles and calves, corsets were flung aside, and dresses became loose and free, all the better to shimmy and shake.

As they do today, early entertainers of all colors found their style within the Black community, and in a back-and-forth exchange, the Black community in turn fed off and expanded upon the looks entertainers wore on stage, on screen, and at their public appearances.

Beyoncé's exquisite *Lemonade* video-opera features several examples of Black style familiar to African Americans. By donning these various styles in her powerful videos and on stage, she fertilizes the growth of trends like goddess braids, Afros, and New Orleans Creole style, among other grace notes.

Yet, despite being surrounded by Black style, we often miss its beauty and innovation or fail to acknowledge it. In this book, I seek to document and represent how Black style is put together and worn, how it is presented, and how it has influenced fashion in ways both large and incremental. My intention was not to make a comprehensive or definitive volume; it is meant to be a fun, informative, and entertaining journey through Black style. ■

OPPOSITE Rihanna at the Council of Fashion Designers Awards in 2014, when she received her well-deserved Fashion Icon Award.

FOLLOWING SPREAD Brit-born Naomi Campbell, global icon and idol, with a much coveted set of Louis Vuitton luggage.

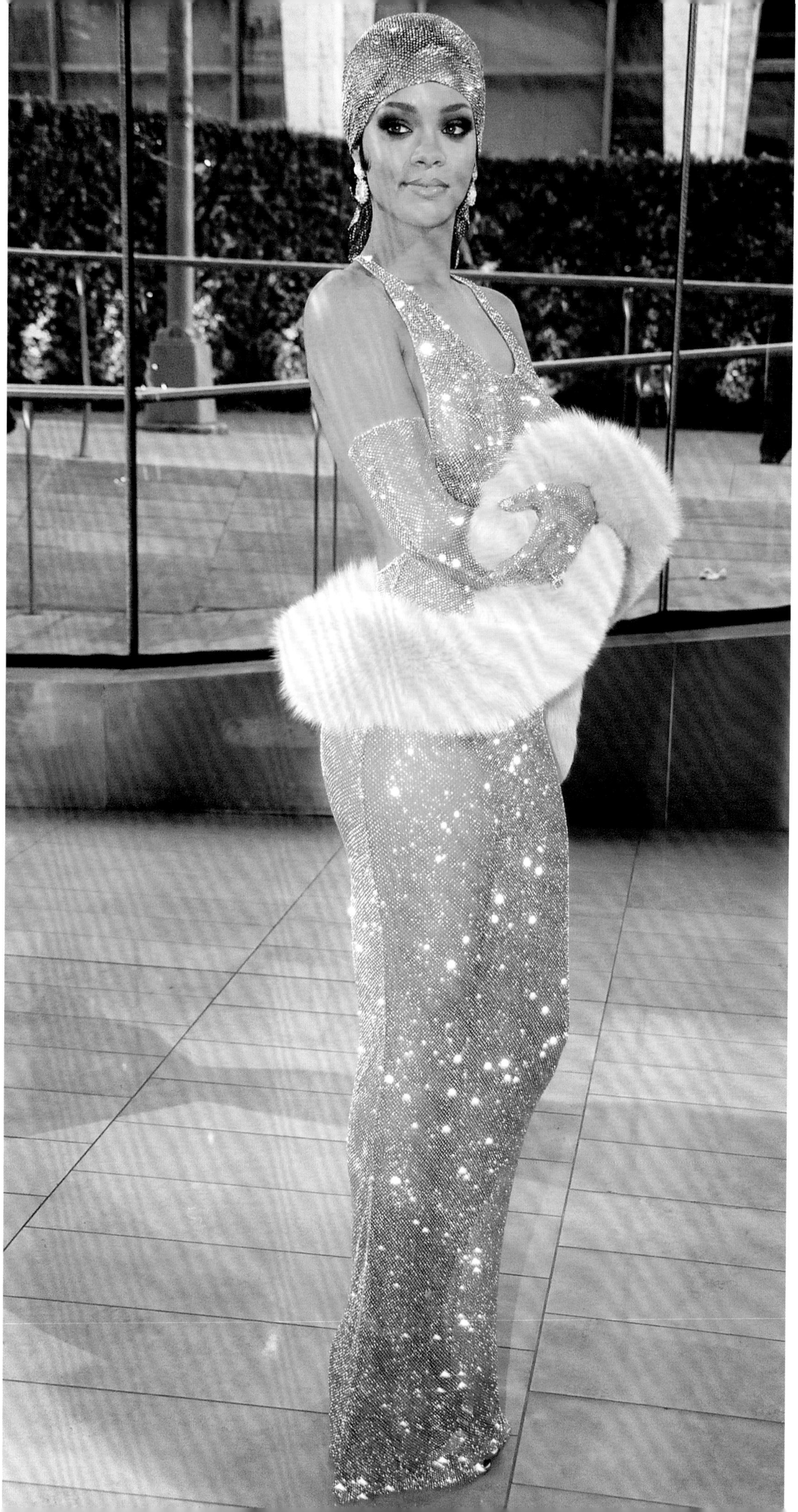

chapter one

ORIGINAL DIVAS

Style for me—Black style, that is—started with my mother, Hazel White. When I was growing up, I didn't know she was turning my brain inside out over style. My mother placed a premium on education: What went into the heads of my three brothers, my sister, and me was more important than what went on our bodies. This engendered in me a feeling that it was unseemly to care much about clothes.

But what a shoe collection she had! I accepted the paradox of a mother who emphasized intellectual pursuits while clearly being obsessed with shoes. I remember the rows of shoes on the wooden stand in her bedroom. God, how I wish I had those shoes now. Shoes that didn't fit in that humble little shoe house stood on the floor of her modest wardrobe or were packed away in her metal trunk.

With the exception of the brown shoes she wore with her brown nurse's uniform, her shoes were exquisite. A sky-high, spindle-heeled pair was the color of Chinese red lacquer. The open toe connected tenuously with delicate cordlike straps that looked as if they would burst on the walk from the car in the driveway to the front door. Chocolate brown pumps, or "court shoes," as my mother called them, had a medium stacked heel and a vamp of leather and a fabric that resembled crochet. Another pair was fashioned from lustrous navy peau de soie with swirling embroidery in the same hue all over the shoe. That sounds genteel; it was not. It was a daring cockroach-killer of a shoe with a staggeringly sharp heel and a vicious pointed toe. Those shoes could have inflicted serious harm. They were fabulous.

OPPOSITE Paris went crazy for the innovative Josephine Baker, who marketed a line of her own hair pomades and skin-darkening creams to women who wanted to look like Baker.

The thing is, I don't recall mother wearing those shoes at all. They just sat there on the shelf, except for a pair of flat sandals in navy leather as soft as "buttah," as Donna Karan would say. The navy was punctuated by white topstitching with long navy and white strings that laced up the leg. These I do remember her wearing. They were the finish to a sporty white sailor suit with tight white bell-bottom pants and a navy and white tunic top.

As a child, I loved to see my mother get glamorous and ebullient in this outfit, but later it seemed to me that she didn't dress up as much after she and my father divorced. Money—the lack of it—and the blues were probably the culprits. One season years later, when she had rebounded and was back in her fashion swing, I took her with me to the Paris shows.

I earned my fashion stripes one *WWD* story at a time. My mother seemed to have been born with hers. That she would be attending the Paris shows was to her the most natural thing in the world. She packed at least a dozen head-to-toes with more changes than Beyoncé onstage at the at the Meadowlands. Then Bill Cunningham noticed her outside the shows. Oh my. From then on, they had their dance each day. She would look out for Bill. He would "accidentally" catch sight of her. She would pose. He egged her on, delighted to see not only what she was wearing, but how she wore it. They reveled in the routine.

Without telling me, she had brought a few wigs with her. She would change them out, depending on the outfit. I remember one outfit—a multi-patterned dress with a blue, white, and gold print and a plunging neckline, gold sandals on her feet. She topped the ensemble with a feathery brown wig, which she wrapped with a metallic gold belt that she used as a hairband, Twenties style.

Bill captured her wide smile as she exited a show and moved through the Louvre like the diva she was, hand cocked in the air, hip pushed to one side. She slayed that day. The attitude, the glamour, the improvisation. This was the very spirit of Black style.

OPPOSITE RiRi, otherwise known as Rihanna, has had a major influence on style, appearing on dozens of magazine covers. This image was the cover of the April 2016 issue of *Vogue*.

Divas like my mother hold a special place in the Black style lexicon. A diva possesses this ineffable something, this attitude. Significant to the diva is presentation. The diva carries herself with aplomb. How she looks and what she wears is of great importance. A diva is seasoned by life and she has a penchant for the dramatic in her clothes and in her actions. (She gets spinach stuck in her teeth when she takes this theatricality too far, but that's another book.)

Divas are admired for their style and vision, for their accomplishments and willingness to expect the best for themselves and for others. Throughout history they've stood as beacons of style. They are women (and occasionally men) like Bessie Smith, Billie Holiday, Josephine Baker, and Dorothy Dandridge. Contemporary divadom extends to Serena and Venus Williams, Erykah Badu, Diana Ross, Tina Turner, Jessye Norman, Grace Jones, the late Whitney Houston, Oprah Winfrey, and diva princesses like Beyoncé, Rihanna, and Lauryn Hill.

And the males? Luther Vandross was famously a diva in his day, and Kanye West earned the title with his passion for fashion and grand visions, not to mention his notable talents.

But what's beautiful about divadom in African-American culture is that anyone who can carry him or herself with confidence and turn their particular style of glamour up to high wattage can earn the sobriquet *diva* for the day. ∎

OPPOSITE Grace Jones in the 1980s embodied beauty and daring.

OPPOSITE Roberta Flack "killed them softly" with her songs and earthy look. Soon after this afro, her braids became a signature look.

FOLLOWING SPREAD LEFT Actor Pam Grier shot to stardom in the early 1970s when she starred in such films as *Foxy Brown*, *Coffy*, and *Sheba, Baby*. Blaxploitation movies, as they are sometimes called, were virtual runways of extravagant Seventies style.

FOLLOWING SPREAD RIGHT Activist and professor Angela Davis, a seminal figure in the 1960s civil rights movement, sported afros of many lengths.

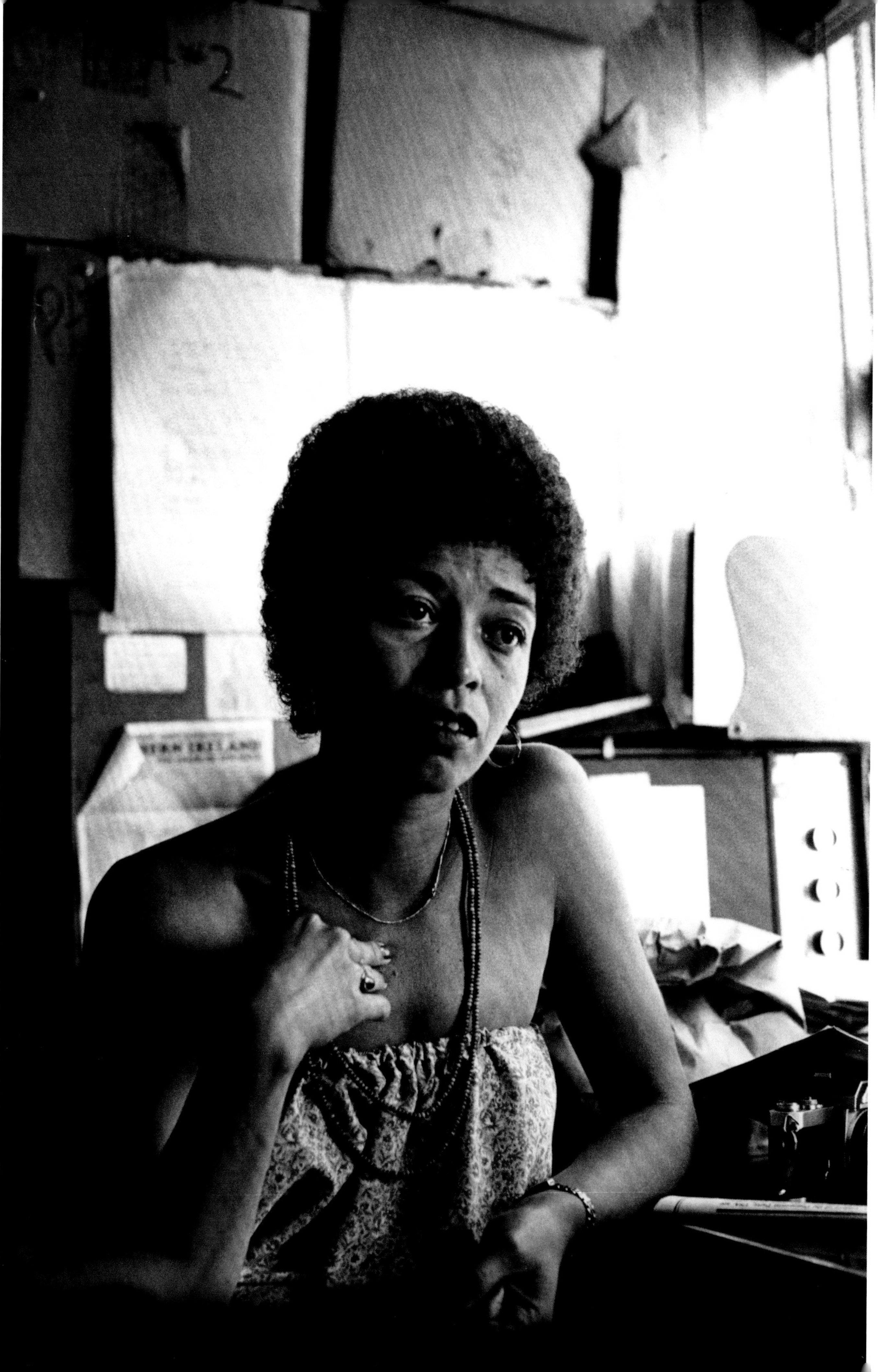

OPPOSITE Beyoncé
Knowles, or Queen Bey,
was a member of Destiny's
Child and has been her
own force of one since
2006. Two watershed
fashion moments were
her 2016 Super Bowl
performance and the
video art piece *Lemonade*.

RIGHT Halle Berry at
the 2002 Academy Awards
when she won the Oscar
for Best Actress for her
role in *Monster's Ball*.
Her red carpet style and
pixie haircut inspired
many women.

ABOVE "Empress" Bessie Smith was the most popular and glamorous female blues singer during the 1920s and 1930s.

OPPOSITE According to a friend, Billie Holiday started wearing white flowers onstage when she burned her hair with curling tongs right before a performance. To cover the burned spot, she wove some gardenias into her hair and never stopped wearing them.

OPPOSITE The audacity of Diana Ross comes through in this image of her in a Bob Mackie design for the film *Mahogany*, mid-1970s. Tom Ford has cited Ross as a major inspiration.

ABOVE Opera diva Leontyne Price.

OPPOSITE Diahann Carroll as we've rarely seen her—in a fierce afro, ca. 1970s.

FOLLOWING SPREAD LEFT Whitney Houston was a muse to Versace.

FOLLOWING SPREAD RIGHT Model, author, and businesswoman Naomi Sims was the first Black model to appear on the cover of *Ladies' Home Journal* in 1968, and on the cover of *Life* in 1969. She was the first supermodel with a dark chocolate complexion, and her eponymous line of wigs grew into a hugely successful beauty empire in the Seventies.

chapter two

Folks can get didactic about Afro-style. It's hard to define due to its breadth and complexity. There are the Holland cloth, the freedom hair, the cornrows, the cowrie shells, the liberation colors. And there are those who would insist that if there's no kente cloth within a mile of it, it ain't Black style. But that's not true. There's the spirit of it. The sexiness. The swag. The baseball cap, snapped back. Jay-Z. Painted-on jeans worn with knee-high boots and big gold hoop earrings were at one point the uniform of Black women in every American city. A fresh pair of Air Jordan high tops plus baggy FUBU jeans and a zigzag fade add up to a uniquely and distinctly Afro style, no matter who's rocking them.

All kinds of people—Black folks, White folks, Nigerian folks, American folks, English, French, and Sudanese—are highly opinionated about Black style. It can be provocative. Black style is personal, but also political. In the Sixties, Afros were considered the hairstyle of revolt. Today, many Black women believe wearing an Afro will impede their career success. Some people may even consider an Afro threatening.

Yet Black style is beautiful, intellectual, and inspiring. It is, sometimes, all-out eccentric even while it is brilliant. It's called *laid*. Someone who's laid is totally put together. Sharp. Someone who's laid has poured a lot of time and effort into looking good, and it's a pleasure to drink in the beauty it embodies. To call someone laid is the highest expression of admiration, an acknowledgment of the lengths that a person will go to achieve that style and nail a look. Laid is also Uncle Willie in a purple suit, ostrich skin loafers, *Super Fly* hat, and pinkie ring, or Cousin Marcia, who after six hours emerged from the hair salon with three different hairstyles on her head. I think of laid and I conjure up all the varied ways Black people just bring "it"—that is, the style. ■

FOLLOWING SPREAD A fashion story from the 1970s when African-American street style was looked to for ideas.

OPPOSITE Sudanese model Alek Wek set standards for style and beauty in the Nineties that still reverberate today.

LEFT Singer-actor Janelle Monáe's original style was sculpted from her penchant for wearing utilitarian outfits with a palette limited mostly to black and white, an homage to her working-class parents.

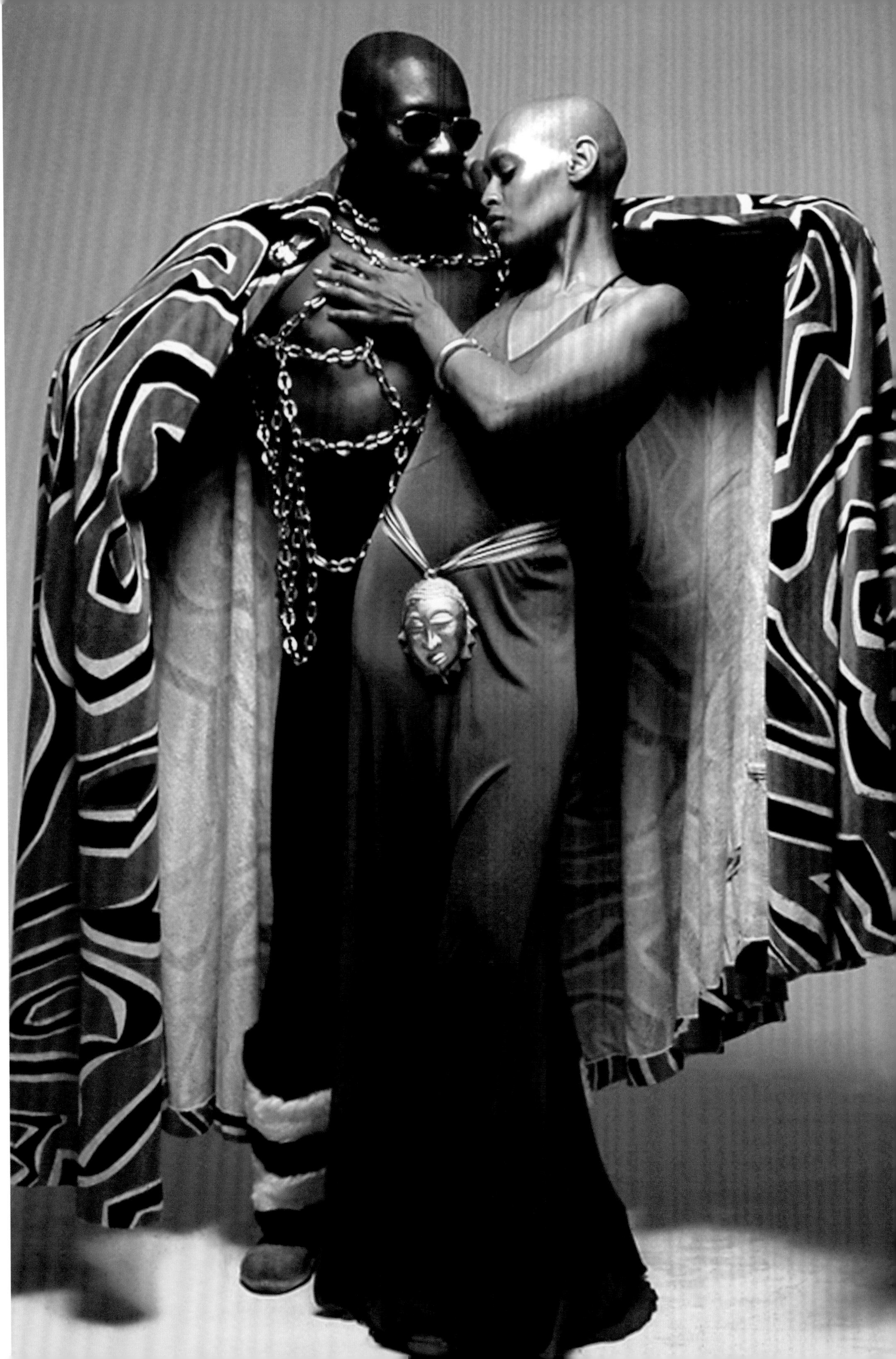

OPPOSITE + ABOVE Isaac Hayes, also known as the Dark Prince, and model Pat Evans in the 1970s. On Pat Evans, a jeweled pendant inspired by a Yoruba mask. Hayes's chains with adinkra links represent the connection to Yoruba and other West African communities where adinkra symbols are important cultural motifs. Twenty years after Hayes, heavy gold chains were adopted by African Americans in the hip hop movement.

OPPOSITE 1970s model Pat Evans shaved her head to draw attention to prejudice in the beauty industry against certain types of hair, and to make the point that we are not defined by our hair.

FOLLOWING SPREAD Television personality, actor, producer, budding fashion mogul, and author Alani Nicole "La La" Anthony.

PREVIOUS SPREAD Fur has long played a central role in Black style. James McQuay was the most renowned of Black furriers in the Seventies and Eighties, but Harlem designer and retailer Daniel Day, known as Dapper Dan, was highly original in his work with fur and thus helped shape hip hop style.

LEFT Naomi Campbell, ca. 1990s. Campbell was, and still is, a major touchstone of fashion and pop culture.

OPPOSITE B-girl and fly-girl fashion emanated from the Eighties.

chapter three

EBONICS

There are those who give voice to Black style.

For decades singers and actors have slayed it with fashion in their videos, on the red carpet, on the stage, and on magazine covers. They would emerge from their black cars and take the street as if it were their own private runway.

Gabrielle Union rocked goddess braids with a sexy caftan, and Beyoncé mixed African-American heritage (Cajun) style with French high-fashion style in the video for "Formation," which was brilliant and original, the centuries old marriage of French and African peoples and culture in the low country notwithstanding.

Lupita Nyong'o has greater significance than a man landing on the moon. To bring it down to earth a bit: Nyong'o's ascension on the scene is akin to actors Pam Grier and Tamara Dobson's emergence during the blaxploitation film era. Her arrival has been justly lauded by people all over the world as a welcome breakthrough, similar to the way Beverly Johnson landing the cover of *Vogue* sent ripples of pleasure and affirmation through the Black community.

What these and other talented and fashionable women have done, and what Nyong'o is doing now, is open a space in the western world for all women with dark skin or other features of African-ness to be regarded as equally beautiful, desirable, and influential.

OPPOSITE Even before actor Kerry Washington gained wide recognition as the lead in the television series *Scandal*, she was a favorite of fashion brands and at designer's shows for her cool elegance.

Loudly and proudly, South Africa's Miriam Makeba and America's Nina Simone communicated as persuasively through their Afrocentric aesthetic as they did through their hypnotic music. What they and ordinary women going about their everyday lives put forth is the visual equivalent of Ebonics: flourishes and notes that take the universal language of clothes and add elements that are endemic to Afro-chic. They bring the flava, baby. It's the click in a Makeba song or the soulful "ugh" in a Wilson Pickett tune or the "give it to me two times—uhn, uhn," from Toots and the Maytals' "54-46 That's My Number."

Notes that float from Miles Davis's trumpet and lyrics shaped by Ella Fitzgerald's singular voice, I believe, come from the same creative space as Fitzgerald's glamorous gowns or Davis's many pairs of flamboyant leather pants. With their African/American/Caribbean garb, the I-Threes, Bob Marley's back-up singers (including his wife, Rita, and reggae stars Judy Mowatt and Marcia Griffiths), redefined the objectified role of female singers. And in so doing they spread a look rooted in turbans and flowing skirts, widely adopted by women globally, that still reverberates today.

Fashion and music are tightly bound together in song. Check out rap, R&B, or reggae and you'll get a fashion lesson that you won't get listening to Céline Dion. If you want to know which brands are popular or have street cred in the community, just listen.

Fashion references were once purely descriptive—dresses, socks, pants. Then ska and reggae DJs and singers—male and female—began toasting about their Clarks booties and Travel Fox shoes. In the Seventies, the practice migrated along with immigrants from Jamaica to Brooklyn and the South Bronx, where American rappers picked up the practice from their Americanized Jamaican brethren and began name-checking brands. B-girls and B-boys breakdanced wearing their sporty, athletic looks, but it was Queens rappers Run-D.M.C. who changed the game artistically and financially with their Adidas tracksuits and shell-toe sneakers.

Caribbean and African Americans continued their cross-pollination well into the new millennium, driving the evolution of definitive Black style. Rihanna, Nicki Minaj, and Drake sit atop a vast intermingling of Caribbean- and African-

OPPOSITE Jazz singer and bandleader Cab Calloway wears the oversized jacket with wide lapels and the high-waisted baggy pants of the zoot suit, which became popular in the 1940s.

American pop influences that might mix dance-hall styles with hip hop on one hand, or Rastafarian signifiers with surfer culture on the other.

Minaj adopted the dance-hall style of reggae and the over-the-top glamour of calypso from her native Trinidad. Meanwhile, on several occasions Rihanna has dipped into her Caribbean roots with songs like "Rude Boy" and "Work." Drake's biggest hit to date, the catchy "One Dance," melds Nigerian, Jamaican, and American music. Could the mash-up of styles have been far behind?

Ralph Lauren and Tommy Hilfiger are accessible and aspirational. Both designers have been favorite labels of the hip hop community and have reaped millions of dollars in sales as a result. But if you're a rapper you have to up your game at every moment; the whole ASAP crew is nipping at your heels. Jay-Z's music is now classic—perhaps that's why he decided to rhyme about one unattainable designer. What does it mean to dedicate an entire song to a designer whose creations most of your young, impressionable fans will never be able to afford? It's the culmination of the trend that began as a validation and a celebration of working-class African-American lifestyle. The designer happened to be Tom Ford, the man who transformed Gucci from passé Italian label to juggernaut. Ford, a native Texan and former actor in television commercials, then started his own eponymous line, and Black men were some of his most devoted patrons. Rich Black men, that is. A Ford suit can be equal in price to a small car; owning one is a mark of discernment, the ultimate fashion medal. It's a beautiful suit. But contrast Jay-Z's song with the tribute neo-soul singer India.Arie composed to celebrate the beauty of Black women's natural hair. That became an international hit , as did Jay-Z's song— strong evidence that Black fashion's arms are spread wide. ■

OPPOSITE Janelle Monáe's style and hair have evolved into more varied choices. The actor and singer landed roles in the films *Moonlight* and *Hidden Figures*, both of which received Oscar nominations in 2017. *Moonlight* won the Oscar for Best Picture.

ABOVE The one and only Mary J. Blige. From fly girl to glamorous chanteuse, she influenced two generations.

OPPOSITE Early on in her career, singer-songwriter, record producer, multiple Grammy winner, and style influencer Alicia Keys garnered attention for her beaded braids. Afrocentric turbans and a boho look have also long been in her arsenal.

FOLLOWING SPREAD LEFT From left: Lisa "Left Eye" Lopes, Rozonda "Chilli" Thomas, and Tionne "T-Boz" Watkins of TLC epitomized Southern hip hop style, 1996.

FOLLOWING SPREAD RIGHT Gorgeous singer Lauryn Hill, seen here in 1998, was one of the most important late century fashion figures and a godmother of present day afro bohemian fashion.

PREVIOUS SPREAD
LEFT In Queens in
the 1980s, the Saint
Albans and Hollis boys,
like LL Cool J, set style
trends. The definitive
accessories: Kangol
hat, dookie chains,
dope ring, earring, and
boom box.

PREVIOUS SPREAD
RIGHT MC Hammer's
iconic harem pants
from the 1980s returned
two decades later as a
reference for drop-crotch
pants and baggy joggers.

LEFT Appropriation and
assimilation: Miley Cyrus
in grills, flamboyant nail
tips, and rapper body
language .

77

chapter four

AFRO-CHIC

fro-chic is the American expression of African style. It is essentially the love child of African and European influences—East meets West. You might catch some of the best looks at the increasingly frequent Afro-punk festivals in Brooklyn and elsewhere, or on celebrities like Solange Knowles who wear African dress from countries such as Uganda, Nigeria, Ghana, and Mozambique. A long dashiki dress, a kente-cloth bow tie, or an ankh pendant carved from gold or wood is a recognizable and iconic fashion from the motherland.

Mother Maya Angelou had something to say about that. This should come as no surprise, as she was an acute observer and statuesque wearer of Black style, from her lithesome days in her youth well into her queenly golden years. Angelou always epitomized Afro-chic. One day she would be in a bold wax-print head-wrap; on another occassion she'd choose a simple, knee-length dress in a dark color and strands of pearls to complement her charming Afro.

Angelou was profoundly affected by Africa. She lived in Ghana for a brief time in the early Sixties and traveled frequently to the continent as a writer and activist. Adopting the local dress of whatever country she was visiting, being the style-conscious fashion maven that she was, she grafted African style onto her American style, creating a singular look of Afro-chic fierceness.

Angelou might have been mulling over the flourishing of African-derived style from Mama Africa and how it is worn by the Black Diaspora, or she could have been thinking about how to put yourself together to slay, when she wrote the following passage: "Seek the fashion which truly fits and befits you. You will always be in fashion if you are true to yourself, and only if you are true to yourself." That quote captures the idea of personal style through the lens of Black culture's most eloquent griot. ■

OPPOSITE Exquisite metal work and beading on supermodel Joan Smalls.

ABOVE Author, dancer, speaker, and activist Maya Angelou often wrapped her hair and her tall, lithesome frame in African style.

OPPOSITE An African king, from the Akuffo family of Ghana, in an early twentieth-century photograph, is swathed in gold, kente cloth, and leopard skins.

Portrait Oumou Diané – 1965 Pose avec no fleur. Malick Sidibé 2008

ABOVE + OPPOSITE Malick Sidibé was known for his stylish black-and-white portraits of everyday people on the streets of Bamako, Mali, taken in the 1960s in his makeshift studios.

FOLLOWING SPREAD Dassanech husbands and their wives in ceremonial garb in Ethiopia.

Portrait au Studio.   1969   Malick Sidibé [signature]   2008

⬛⬛⬛⬛⬛ Dancers wearing leopard skins in the Muyinga province of Burundi, ca. 1971. Leopard skins are long-standing symbols of royalty and wealth.

⬛⬛⬛⬛⬛⬛⬛⬛ Maverick rapper and fashion princess Nicki Minaj attends New York Fashion Week in 2015.

OPPOSITE Naomi Campbell in an African-inspired dress. She has been photographed by every major fashion photographer of the last thirty years.

FOLLOWING SPREAD LEFT A dress by Cameroonian Paris-based designer Martial Tapolo at Dakar Fashion Week in Senegal, 2014.

FOLLOWING SPREAD RIGHT The cowry shells around the model's neck and on her embroidered dress were once used as currency in Africa. They are also symbols of womanhood, fertility, and birth.

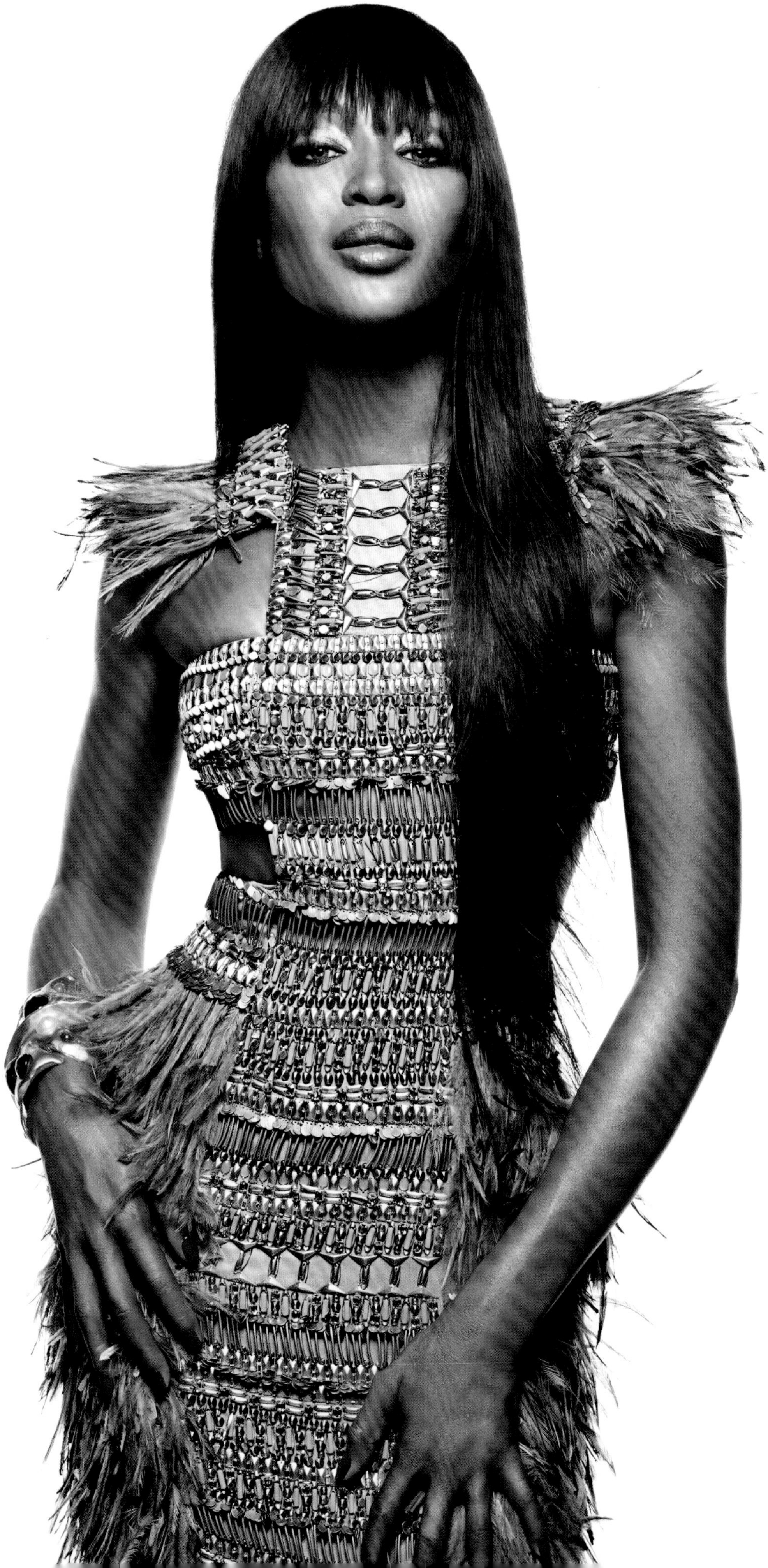

OPPOSITE Caftan and afro style from the 1970s.

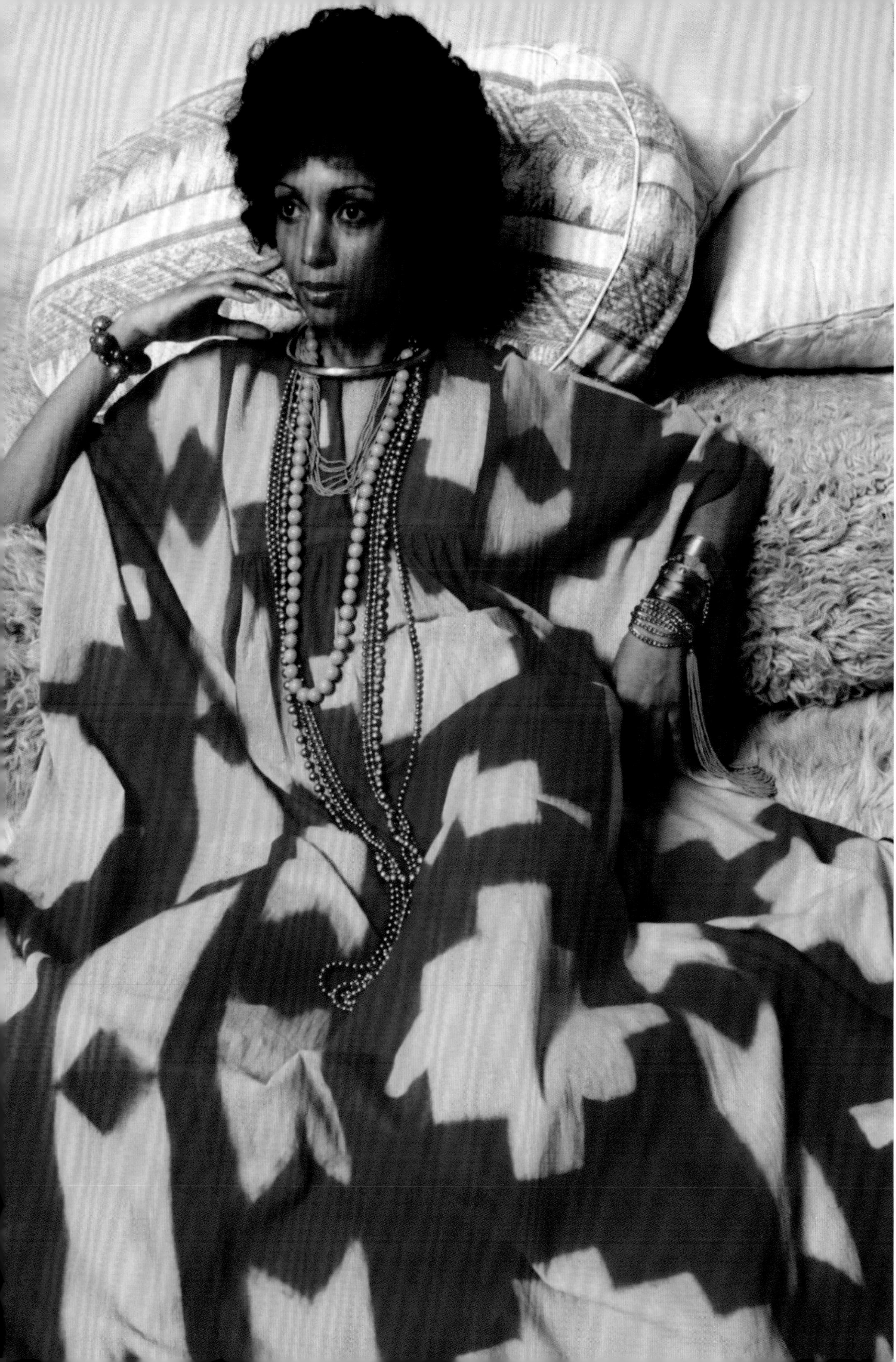

Cutting edge Italian
designer Romeo Gigli set the
pace for high fashion in the
late 1980s and early 1990s
with a wave of romanticism.
He incorporated Bogolan
and Muslim fabrics; soft,
unstructured shapes; and
West African beading in
his designs.

RIGHT Velvet-voiced Luther Vandross at his home in Greenwich, Connecticut, 1998.

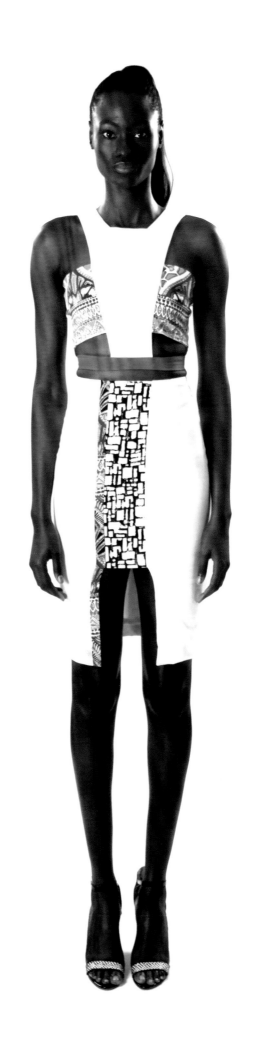

OPPOSITE South African singer and activist Miriam Makeba, ca. 1970, inspired women worldwide to wear African clothes and close cropped afros, which became known as "makebas."

RIGHT The groundbreaking website Zuvaa is a rich resource for Afro-inspired style.

LEFT Afro meets Anglo in clothing from Zuvaa.

OPPOSITE Bright colors, beads, and Aso-oke prints are characteristic of an intensely African approach that combines indigenous fabrics, Masai Mara jewelry, and a simple Western dress shape.

chapter five

BARE BEAUTIES

When and how much we choose to show our skin is integral to any look. Whether we like it or not, porn has been absorbed into the mainstream, forcing new calibration of how much skin is acceptable to display. In light of this development, it's unsurprising that a modesty movement is gaining traction as a counterpoint to the currency of nudity. Music videos and amateur dance-hall videos have helped shape style, but the fomenting of colorism and the rise of the hoochie-mama look—cleaned up or raw—wield far-reaching impact.

We debate whether or not it's appropriate to treat skin tone as a design element—all White models, or all Black, in a show? Some designers would call it an aesthetic decision. When I hear that, danger signals start exploding in my head.

The color of our skin can be such a hot-button topic that it's sometimes difficult to call it as it is. Some folks don't want to say black or dark skin out of fear of causing offense—because they have been taught there's something offensive about it. They prefer to say chocolate or brown, when in fact we are all brown or beige. Few skin tones are actually black, just as few are actually white. But they are all beautiful, as this poem celebrates. ∎

OPPOSITE Singer-songwriter Nefatari. Queen Nefertari, or "beautiful companion," ruled Egypt with Ramesses the Great in ancient times. The famous African queens—Cleopatra, Nefertiti, and Nefertari—though often portrayed in Western culture as White, continue to inspire.

SKIN

by Constance C. R. White

Her beauty lies in her skin

A polished mahogany

A burnished teak

Brown as a ripe berry

The blue black of a blueberry

I love how dark it is

I love how deep it is

I love how soft it is

I love how olive it is

I love how pale it is

Like...

Like honey

Like sugar

Like molasses

I like how sweet it is

And I remember how tender she is

ABOVE Model Pat Evans in the 1970s.

FOLLOWING SPREAD Actor, musician, and activist Jada Pinkett-Smith. The butt became the focus and was embraced by both sexes in the Nineties through music videos and such designers as Alexander McQueen.

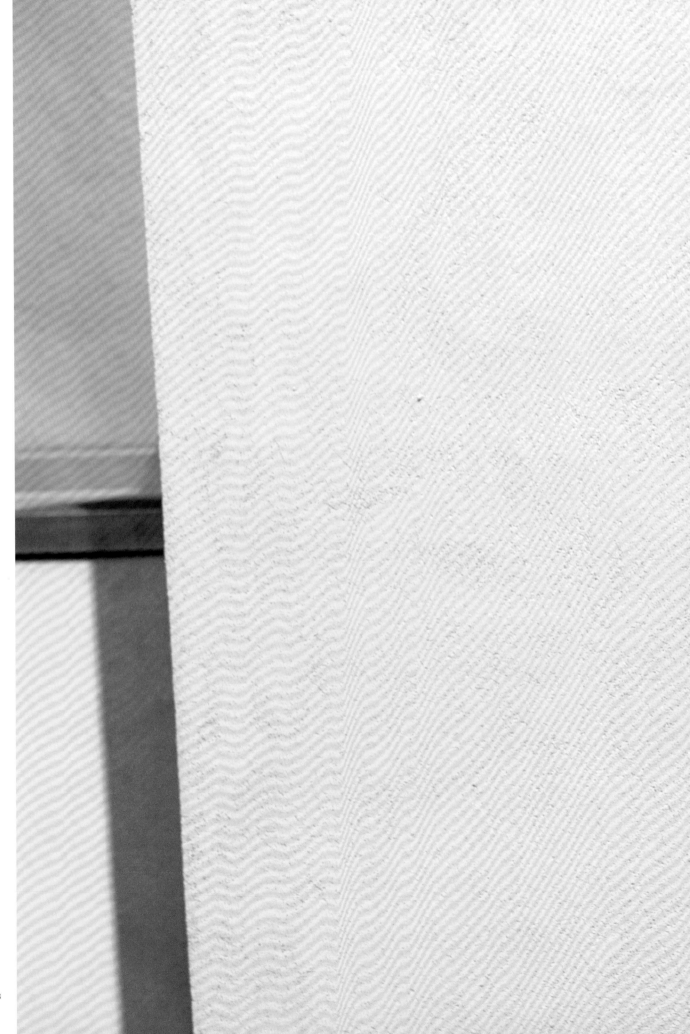

⌐⌐⌐∨⌐ Arriving in Paris in the 1920's, Josephine Baker marcelled her hair, wore a banana skirt, and consorted with the likes of Paul Poiret, a leading fashion designer of the day.

⌐⌐⌐⌐⌐⌐⌐⌐ Model Toukie Smith was both sister and muse to barrier-breaking designer Willi Smith.

RIGHT Alek Wek, 1990s.

OPPOSITE In the James Bond film *Die Another Day*, Halle Berry recreated an iconic scene from the early Bond film *Dr. No*.

FOLLOWING SPREAD Bathing beauties, including model legend Pat Cleveland (third from right), ca. 1970s.

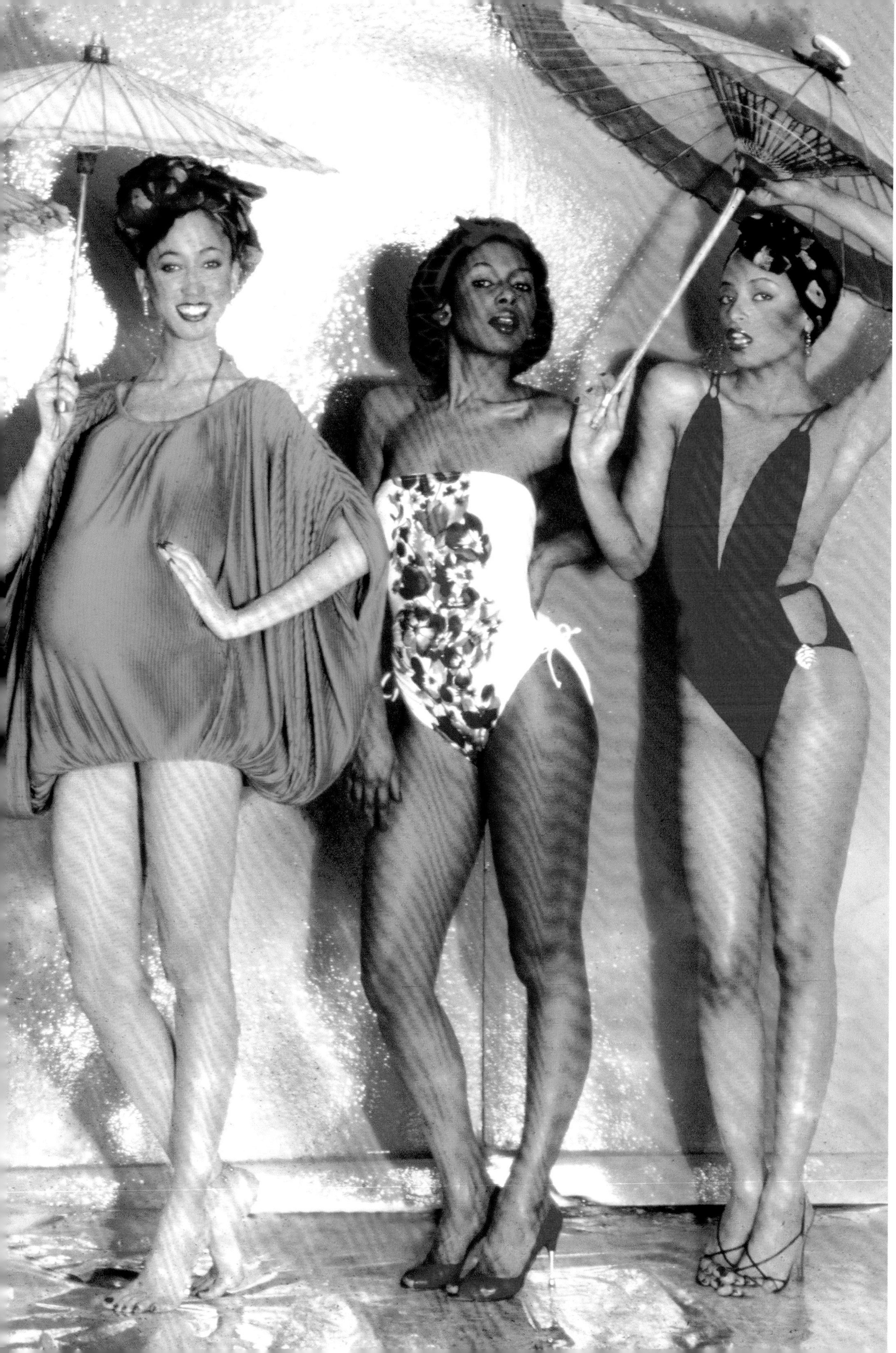

chapter six

NATURAL HAIR
& OTHER CROWNS

Ancient African civilizations viewed the head as the seat of spirituality and leadership, so naturally its coverings were of major symbolic importance. More than any other adornment, a head covering depicted social status. In countries like Ghana, Nigeria, Sudan, Ethiopia, and Kenya, turbans and kufis are worn. Turbans celebrate special occasions, such as birth, marriage, Sunday church, or Muslim worship. Turbans in the right hands—and often those hands are Nigerian—are an art form. The best are quite simply splendid sculptural wonders, elaborate creations wrapped and arranged in three dimensions, soaring out from the head like the plumage of magnificent birds about to take flight.

Today Afros, Afro puffs, locks, cornrows, braids, and Bantu knots are creative Black styles adopted by a variety of races.

The Afro is so cool and singular. This crowning achievement speaks volubly about Black style. It defies gravity; it blooms. It defines Black style. Worn close cropped, it's a sexy, efficient hairstyle that emphasizes the voluptuousness or delicacy of a woman's features. Worn long and free, it's a crown or halo and, for some, a marker of fierce pride. For still others, it's just the latest hairstyle. But its renaissance among women and men alike is indicative of the velocity of growth of the natural hair movement. This movement started about ten years ago and has gained ground among Black women who said "no more" to the damage caused and the time taken to relax their hair permanently.

OPPOSITE The prince of pop and influence, Michael Jackson, seen here in 1977, set off several style trends before and after his multiple plastic surgeries.

Black women describe going natural as both a spiritual and practical journey. And lately it's become something else, too—fashionable.

The women who propelled natural hair forward were the same ones who early on embraced head wraps. It's now wonderfully commonplace to see young Black women on American city streets rocking turbans. I once read a web post by a woman advising her fellow millennials that if it's a man you're looking for, a good man, the turban can be a most effective tool. She maintained that men find women in turbans attractive. She spoke from experience, she said. I'm not judging, but it is possible that a woman in a turban transmits to men—of any race—a certain cultural pride, queenliness, and self-knowledge that's alluring. What is obvious: A good wrap can lift a mediocre outfit and make it a sure-to-slay look.

If on a Sunday you did not see women in their church hats, you'd think you had the wrong day of the week. Sundays, in all communities of the African Diaspora from the United States to England to the Caribbean, have generated a beloved tradition: the church hat, an audacious combination of the temporal and the spiritual. When a church lady gets going with the ritual of selecting a Sunday hat to top off a carefully chosen dress or suit, fall back. This is serious business. It's a unique pleasure to witness how Black women use haute fashion in the service of genuine worship.

The don't-run-your-fingers-through-my-hair look, or the hair weave, was in full swing among Black women even before White hotel heiress Paris Hilton popularized it among White women. In fact, it's now a revenue maker for many men and women in the community, as the sale of hair for weaves has skyrocketed and seems to be holding steady.

Black style's been copied and appropriated. It's been negated and it's made a lot of people plenty of money. Most crucially, however, its silky cords and sturdy cottons weave together a shared history of fashion. This common history strengthens community and Black people's sense of self amid a larger culture.

Without getting into a debate about who does and does not have the right to wear and express Black style, I do want to say a word about cultural appropriation, a topic much on people's minds as Black style's influence grows. I couldn't hold back a half-laugh at Whoopi Goldberg's remark on ABC's show

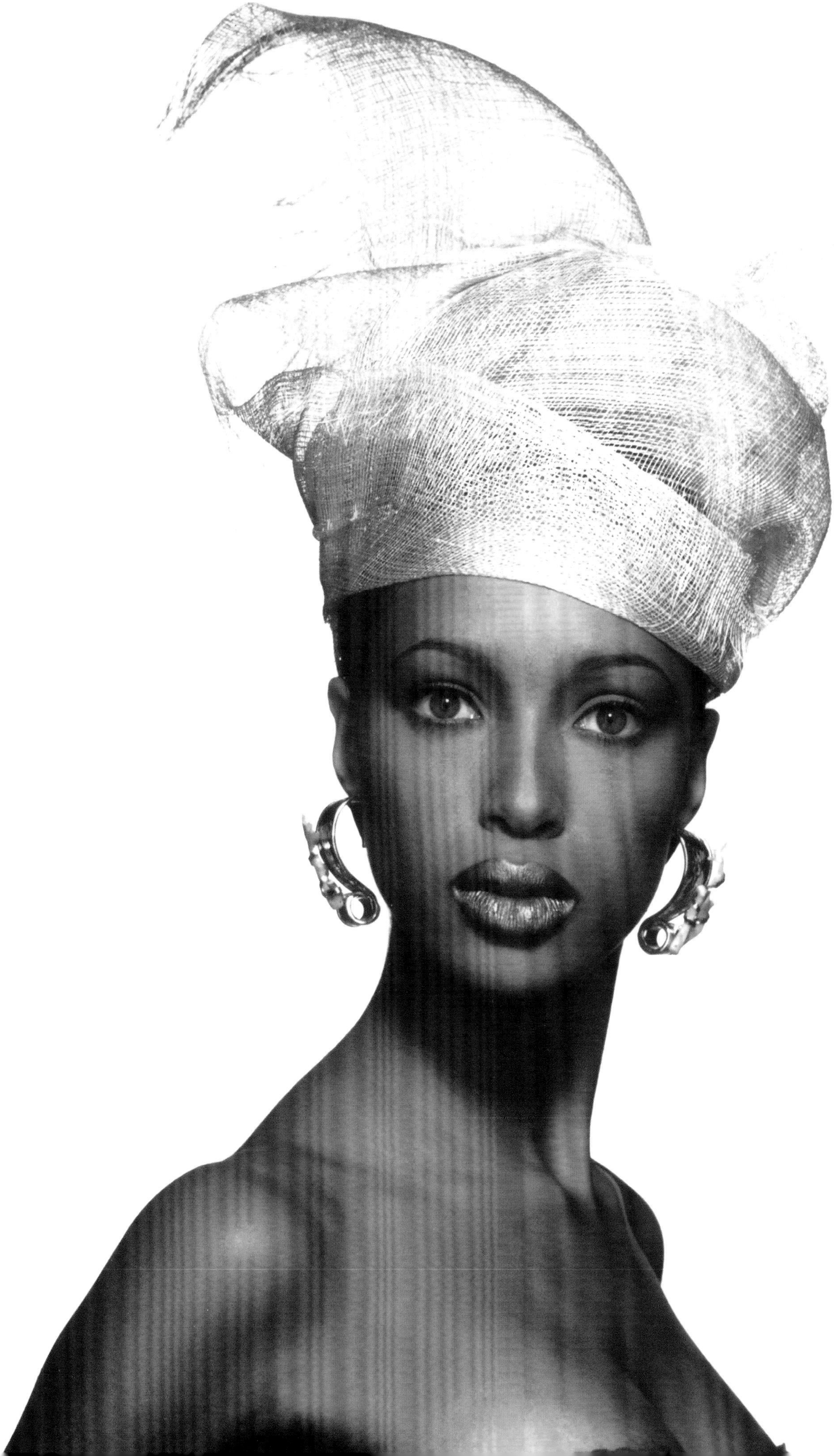

The View that Black women should look at their "White lady hair" before crying appropriation. Perhaps Goldberg meant only to be humorous, but it has to be acknowledged that there's a grain of truth in her comment. However, there is a difference when it comes White appropriation of Black mores and culture. Firstly, there is scant acknowledgment of the origin of the look or behavior that is being appropriated. The source is exploited. In that situation, only one side wins. In 2017 Gucci's creative director Alessandro Michele was exposed through social media for a jacket he designed that is clearly inspired by—many would say a line-by-line copy of—one designed by Daniel Day, aka Dapper Dan, in the 1980s for the Olympic sprinter Diane Dixon. Dapper Dan's Harlem boutique was the cynosure for the popular logo-and-leather look of the day. The second notable difference is having your "stuff" taken without being able to share fully in the collective community that Blacks and Whites built together. The situation is hypocritical and unjust. Still, the idealist in me hopes to see a kumbaya day when there's a free flow of ideas among cultures, and cultural appropriation is replaced by multicultural celebration. ∎

▣▣▣▾▣ No matter the day of the week, the late civil rights leader Dorothy Height was rarely without her "Sunday" hat. Here she is attending a ceremony where she was awarded the Congressional Gold Medal in Washington, DC, 2004.

▣▾▾▣▣▮▣▣ A lady dressed in her best for church on Sunday. Her outfit would not be complete without the crowning glory, a hat with a personality of its own.

OPPOSITE Nina Simone, ca. 1969.

ABOVE A statement hat on Aretha Franklin, the queen of soul.

OPPOSITE Lupita Nyong'o's hairstyle on the red carpet at the Cannes Film Festival in 2015 melded Afrocentric style with Princess Leah buns and the natural hair movement.

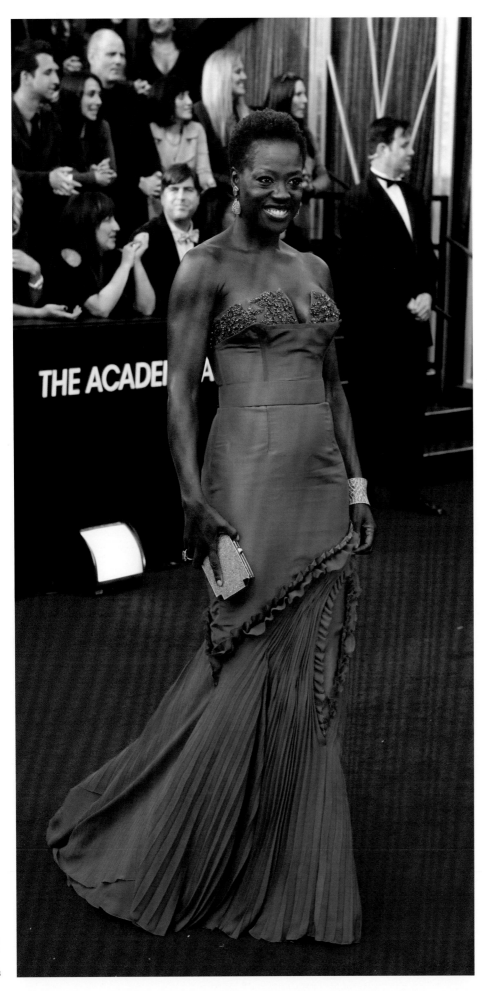

HOW TO WIN

LEFT Actor and producer Viola Davis has evolved into a style arbiter, and is the only Black woman to be nominated for three Academy Awards. She won one in 2017 for Best Supporting Actress for *Fences*.

OPPOSITE Lupita Nyong'o, born of Kenyan parents in Mexico, won the Oscar for Best Supporting Actress for her breakthrough role in *12 Years a Slave* and simultaneously became a major style influencer.

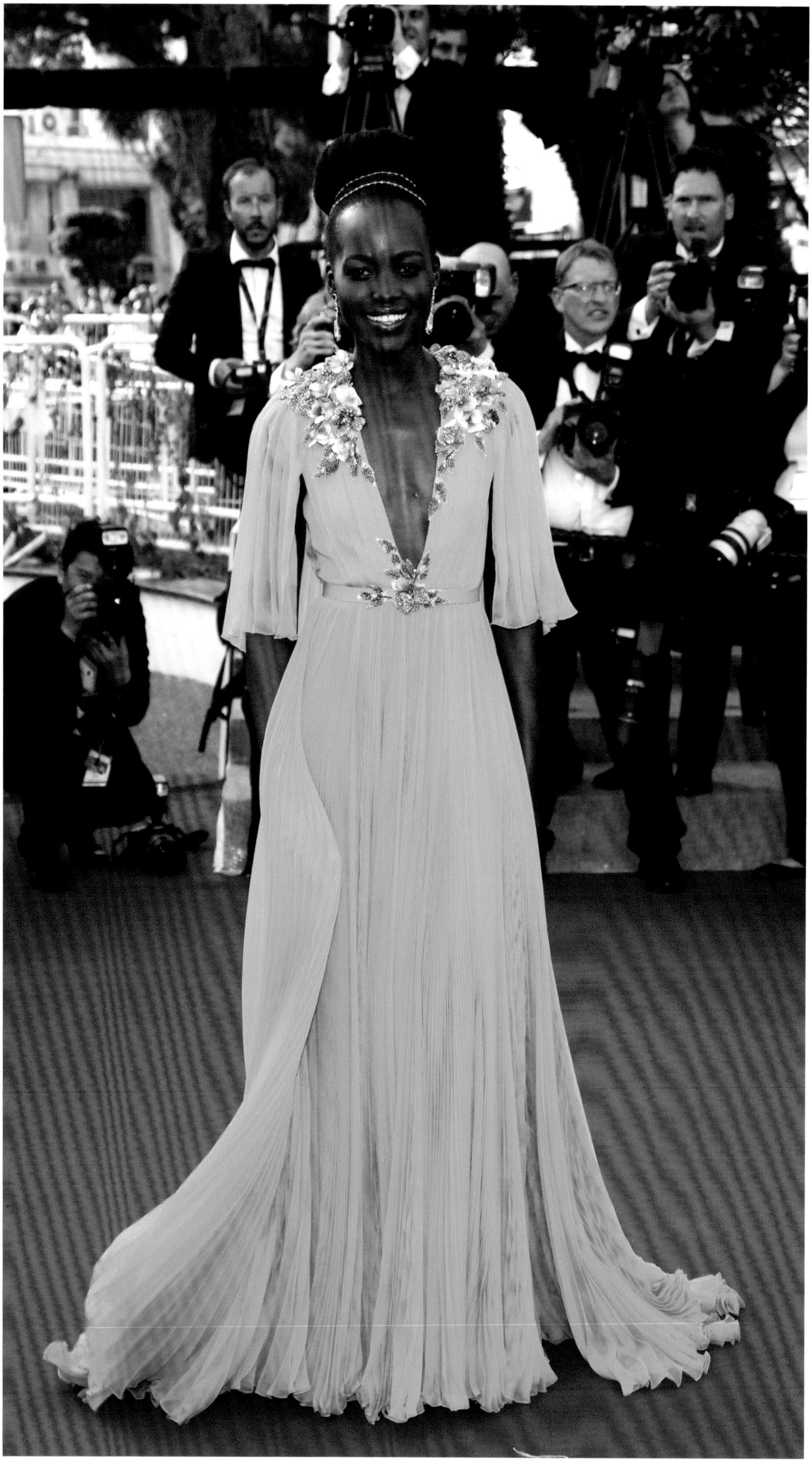

OPPOSITE Afro glory in the 1970s.

ABOVE Afro glory today.

ABOVE Left to right: Judy Mowatt, Rita Marley (Bob Marley's wife and muse), and Marcia Griffiths of the I-Threes set a new standard with their Rastafarian style, seen here onstage in 1977. Bob Marley is second from right.

OPPOSITE Tina Turner in Azzedine Alaïa, the French-Tunisian designer, whom she helped popularize, ca. 1980s.

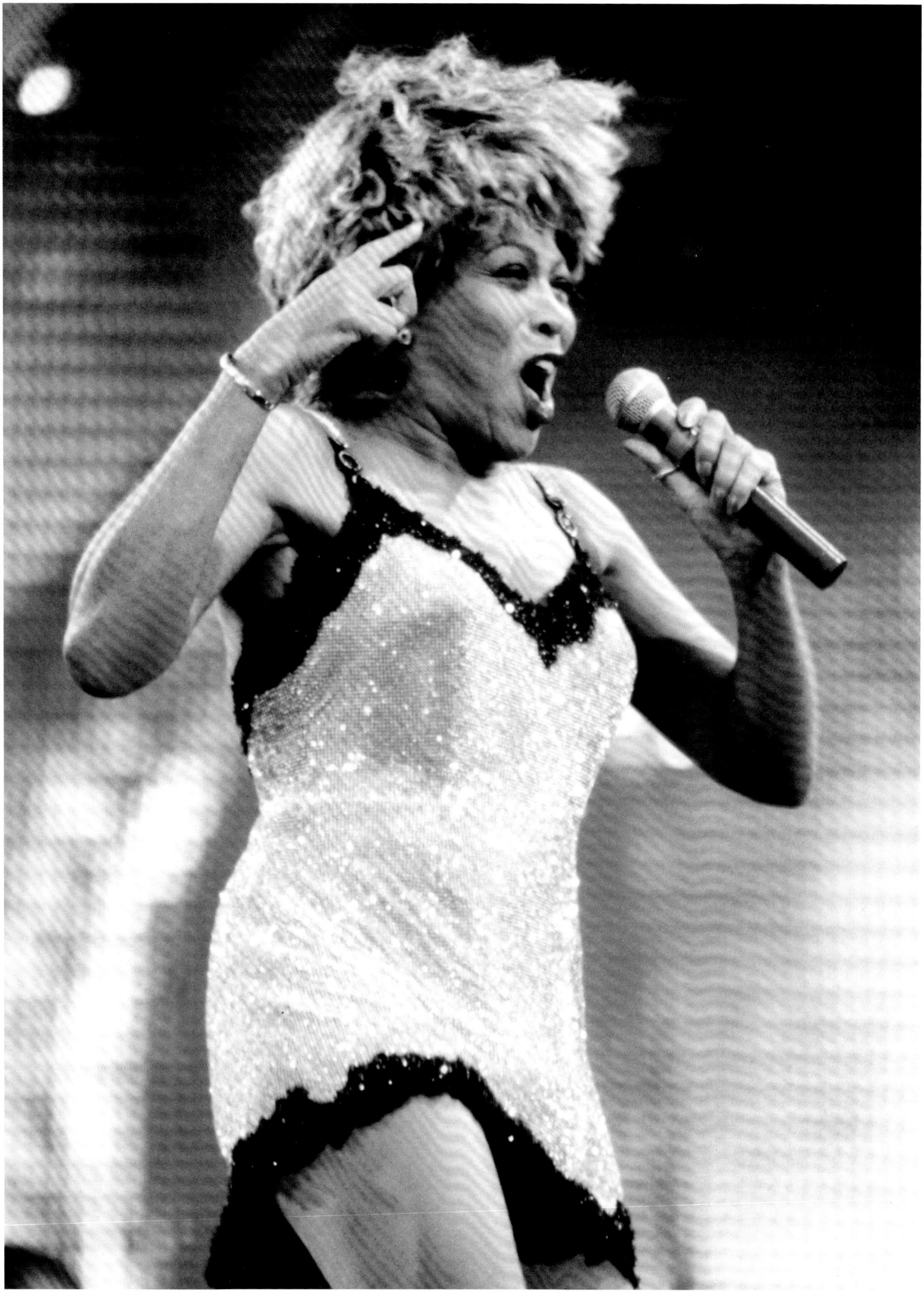

ABOVE A wild-child in her day, fashion influencer Chaka Khan was the queen of funk, ca. 1980s.

OPPOSITE Singer-songwriter, record producer, DJ, and activist Eryka Badu wears "a natural" and multi-finger rings that were popularized by African Americans.

FOLLOWING SPREAD LEFT Microbraids and beads on singing sweetheart Patrice Rushen, ca. 1980.

FOLLOWING SPREAD RIGHT A turban and hoop earrings on Alicia Keys.

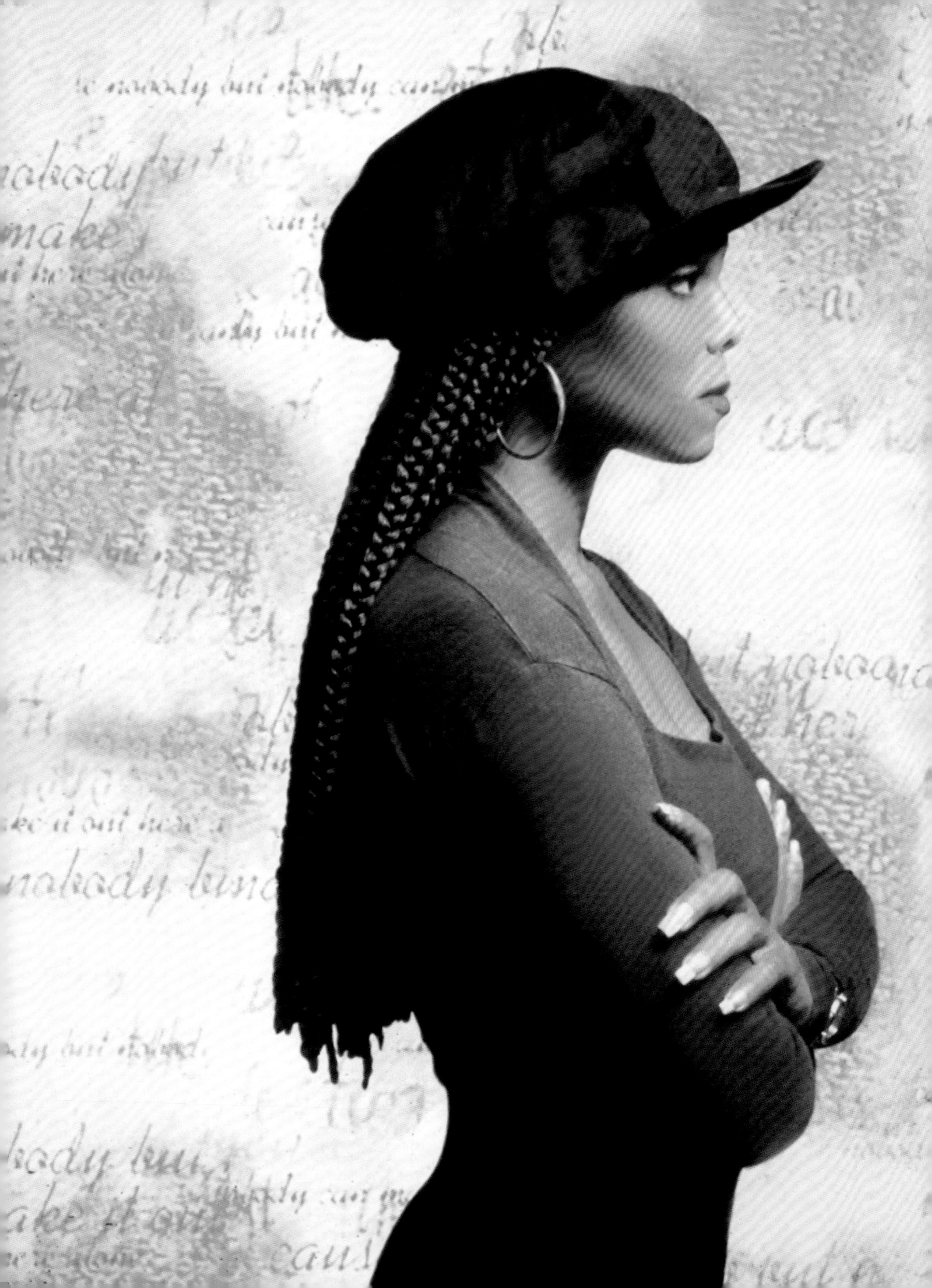

LEFT Janet Jackson in goddess braids for the film *Poetic Justice*, 1993, in which she played the lead.

FOLLOWING SPREAD LEFT Blonde ambition and tattoos on Mary J. Blige.

FOLLOWING SPREAD RIGHT Coretta Scott King talks with a fellow parishioner outside Ebenezer Baptist Church, 1964.

LEFT Sophia Richie, daughter of superstar Lionel Richie, wears cornrows and baby hair—brushing down the delicate hairs around the hairline—which have been historical beauty marks of Black people around the world.

OPPOSITE A modern take on Bantu knots originating in the Bantu communities of southern Africa.

FOLLOWING SPREAD LEFT A kufi hat in Ankara fabric.

FOLLOWING SPREAD RIGHT A model in a beautiful dhuku, or headwrap, and a bib necklace of multiple chains.

142

chapter seven

COUPLES

There have always been women who dress for men. That's part of the dating and mating rituals of humans. It's difficult to imagine a time when this wasn't true. However, this state of affairs has evolved somewhat. One of the central ideas of a blog called *Man Repeller* is documenting a world where women do not dress for men. What's even more interesting is that men are increasingly reversing the roles and dressing for women, but with more transparency.

The look that successfully grabs a man's or a woman's attention depends on the times. In the Forties and Fifties, it might have been the wide-lapel zoot suit and pressed hair on a man. In the Seventies a lush, blazing Afro on a woman could draw a man like bees to honey. The bare-chested crooner onstage was sexy in the rhythm and blues era; in another time, Black women responded to the man in a suit as the embodiment of attractiveness.

For most of the two decades or so that hip hop has existed, style has been unisex. In the last few years, there has been a shift to a more glamorous way of dressing that emphasizes luxury and designer looks and a discrete oppositional masculine/feminine approach to dressing. One of the best examples of this is evidenced by power couple Jay-Z and Beyoncé, whether they're stepping out in Cuba or at the Metropolitan Museum of Art Costume Institute gala. ■

FOLLOWING SPREAD LEFT Emulating 1920s style, in the Nineties, at the Cotton Club in Harlem.

FOLLOWING SPREAD RIGHT Caftans and djellabahs were popular with both sexes in the 1970s.

HOW TO SLAY

ABOVE Jay-Z and Beyoncé on the red carpet of the Met Ball in 2015. They are regulars at this event, the annual fundraiser for the Costume Institute at the Metropolitan Museum of Art.

OPPOSITE Off-screen, Diahann Carroll wore an elegant bourgeois style (here with then-partner British television host and producer David Frost in the early 1970s).

OPPOSITE Naomi Campbell in a *Vogue* shoot with Steve "Blacker Dread" Martin, owner of the legendary Blacker Dread record store, a crucible for Black culture in London, where Campbell grew up.

FOLLOWING SPREAD RIGHT Cynthia Bailey was a successful model strutting runway shows and landing the cover of *Essence*, before she became a television star in *Real Housewives of Atlanta*.

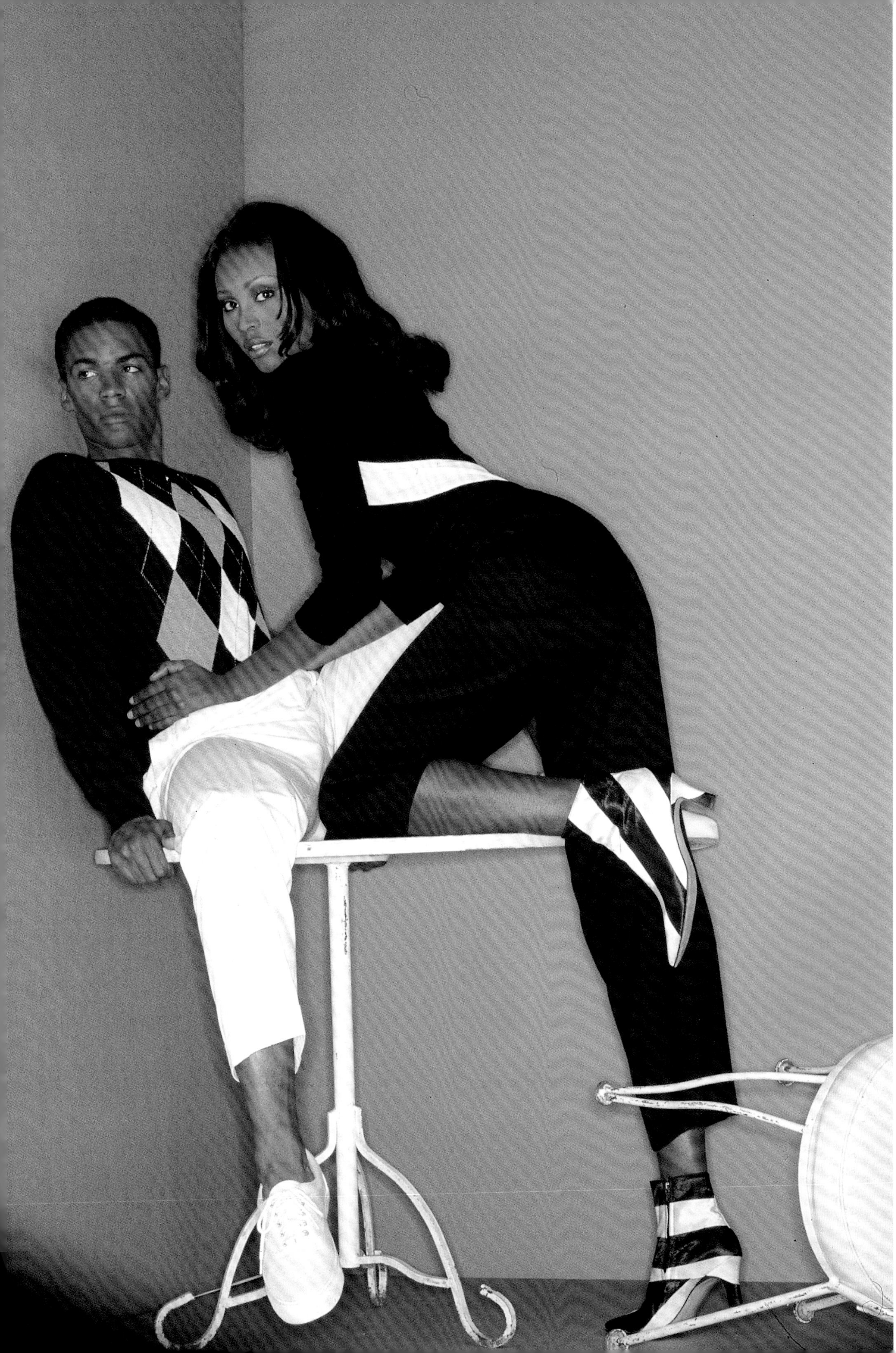

ABOVE + OPPOSITE First Lady Michelle Obama made an irrefutable case for the power of style, championing new talents such as Jason Wu, who designed her white dress (opposite) for the Inaugural Ball in 2009.

SASHAY, SHANTÉ

Q: *So you prefer tall blonde women?*

A: *No. No woman is harder to dress than a Swedish woman. And no woman is easier to dress than a woman of color. So much so, that this season, I have intentionally used fewer black models than usual. They exude so much power, so much elegance; it's wonderful but really too easy. This time I am going to try to do without black models. This will be the winter of blondes.*

—Yves Saint Laurent, from a 1991 interview with *Le Figaro*

Countless ideas emerge from designers' minds, and the best of them are displayed on the runways.

Black and White designers alike explore and plumb African culture for inspiration. I went on a trip to Côte d'Ivoire some years ago to co-produce a fashion show. It ignited a creative spark among designers coming together from both sides of the Atlantic. From America, we took Tracy Reese, Byron Lars, and Edward Wilkerson. From Côte d'Ivoire and other African nations came the talented Alphadi, Lady Mitz, and others. It was exciting to see the two camps collaborate in a show and to see more African-inspired styles on New York runways the following seasons.

Gwen Stefani's predilection for Black style gave her brand a certain je ne sais quoi. Other non-Black designers who have effectively tapped into Afro style include Ralph Lauren, Sophie Theallet, Erin Beatty, and Max Osterweis of the now defunct Suno label, Miuccia Prada, Grace Wales Bonner, Jean-Paul Gaultier, Rifat Özbek, John Galliano, and Catherine Malandrino.

OPPOSITE Robin "Rihanna" Fenty strikes a pose.

Beyond the creative wellsprings of art, geography, fashion, and music, models and beauties of African descent have a history of becoming muses to some of the world's most important designers. The story of the muse as inspirational figure is an extraordinary tale of the power, beauty, and spirit of Black women and designers' willingness to see beyond skin color and race. Included among the most important artist-muse collaborations are Naomi Campbell for Azzedine Alaïa, Iman for Calvin Klein, Mounia Orosemane for Yves Saint Laurent, Toukie Smith for her brother Willi Smith, Pat Cleveland for Stephen Burrows, and Coco Mitchell for Ralph Rucci. Rihanna, Beyoncé, and Zoë Kravitz inspire designers like Alexander Wang, Olivier Rousteing, Stuart Weitzman, and LaQuan Smith. Designers turn again and again to these women, whose faces and bodies represent an ideal of beauty. They have often acted as consiglieri to designers and offered critical and practical feedback on designs. Serving as both conduit and mirror, a muse brings a designer's creations to life.

Photographers and editors have also played an important role in choosing and encouraging muses. Editors may match designers with celebrities, and it is in the interest of both designer and editor for a particular socialite to be seen in a dress featured in the pages or on the website of an editor's magazine. For a gala event, *Vogue* might suggest a fashion theme and help designers find the perfect stars or starlets to project it.

Under the tutelage of legendary editor and fashion maven Eunice Johnson, models like Pat Cleveland and Billie Blair built wildly successful careers and were Black women pioneers in beauty. A muse pushes good photographers further and helps them to realize images that may exist only in their imaginations. Gilles Bensimon and Steven Meisel, among many others, helped shape and have been shaped by the inimitable Naomi Campbell. In the Nineties, Bensimon trained his lens on Tyra Banks and Beverly Peele, exalting their careers and generating some of the era's outstanding images in fashion, including memorable covers for *Elle*.

Two decades ago, Anthony Barboza photographed iconic images of Black style by playing off the beauty of model Pat Evans. More recently the photographer duo of Mert Alas and Marcus Piggott have shot stunning images of model Joan Smalls, among others. The talented pair, who are helping to redefine modern fashion photography, have also photographed Naomi Campbell. After more than two decades at the forefront of the fashion industry, Campbell remains one of the most popular muses among both designers and photographers. Simply put, there is no other like Naomi Campbell. ■

OPPOSITE Stephen Burrows with his muse Pat Cleveland in the 1980s. Burrows engineered the distinctive lettuce-edged jersey and color blocks in slinky dresses that have been widely copied ever since.

Runway model Mounia in the early 1980s. She was one of Yves Saint Laurent's top muses.

LEFT Model, actor, and businesswoman Iman, who was scouted in Somalia as a schoolgirl, brought a sophisticated global style to America.

LEFT Gwen Stefani wears her own L.A.M.B. collection, which draws heavily on Afro-centric culture.

OPPOSITE Rude girl style on the L.A.M.B. runway.

FOLLOWING SPREAD LEFT Designer Kevan Hall finds inspiration in the style of the Ndebele people of Zimbabwe.

FOLLOWING SPREAD RIGHT Jean Paul Gaultier's runway vision, reminiscent of Harlem Renaissance style, on Naomi Campbell.

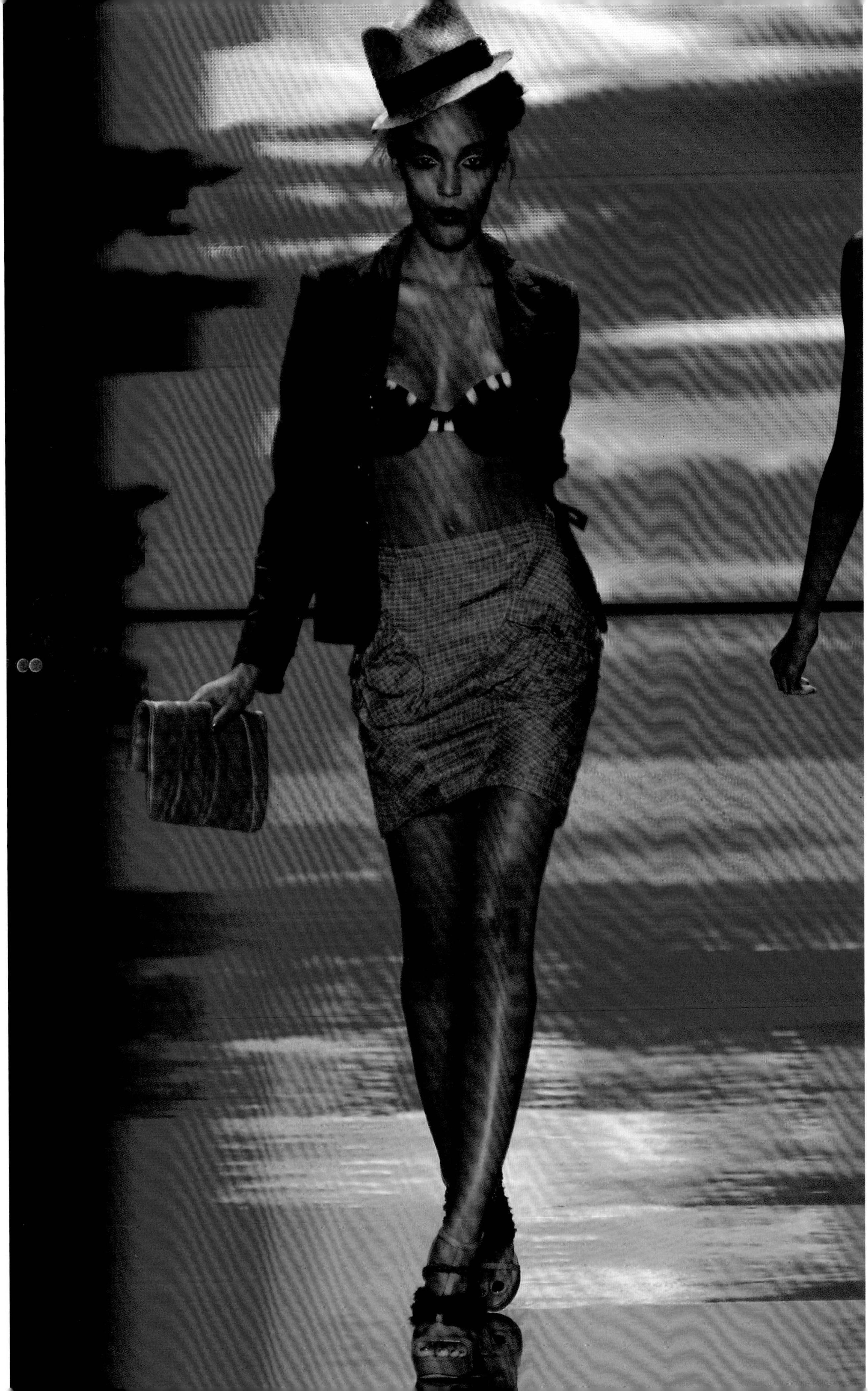

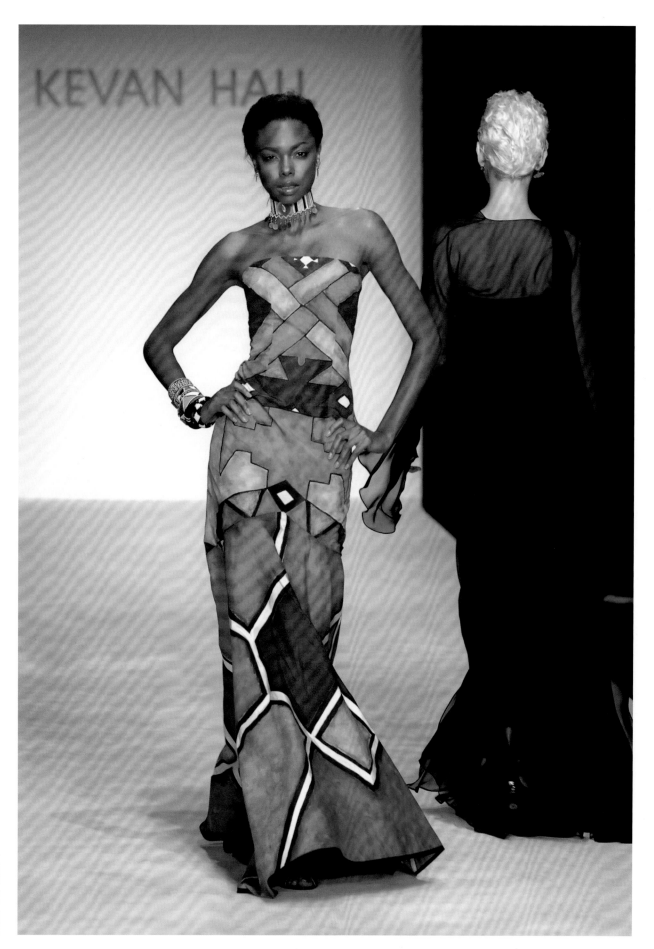

KEVAN HALL

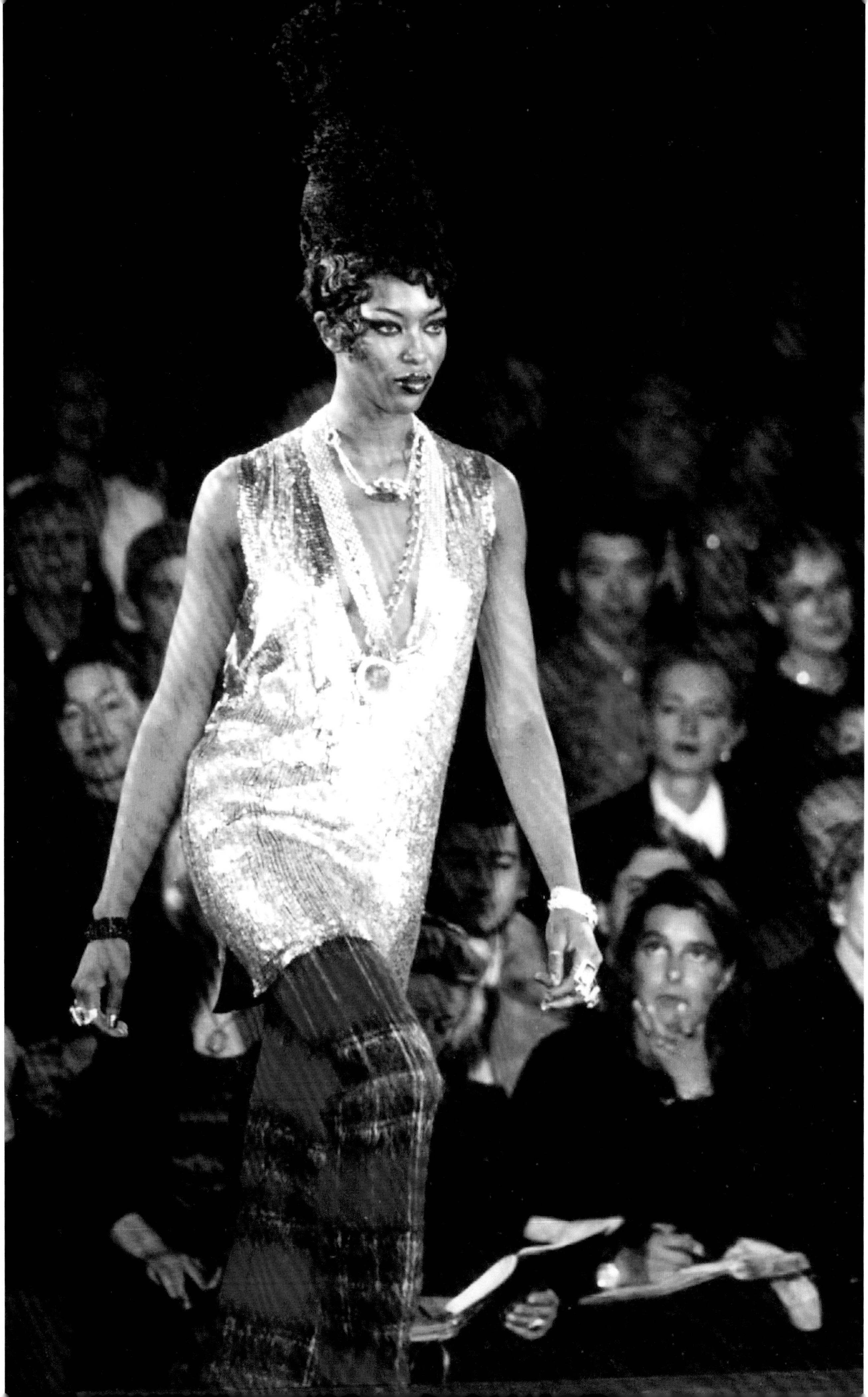

LEFT Designer Sophie Theallet's fierce ode to Black style.

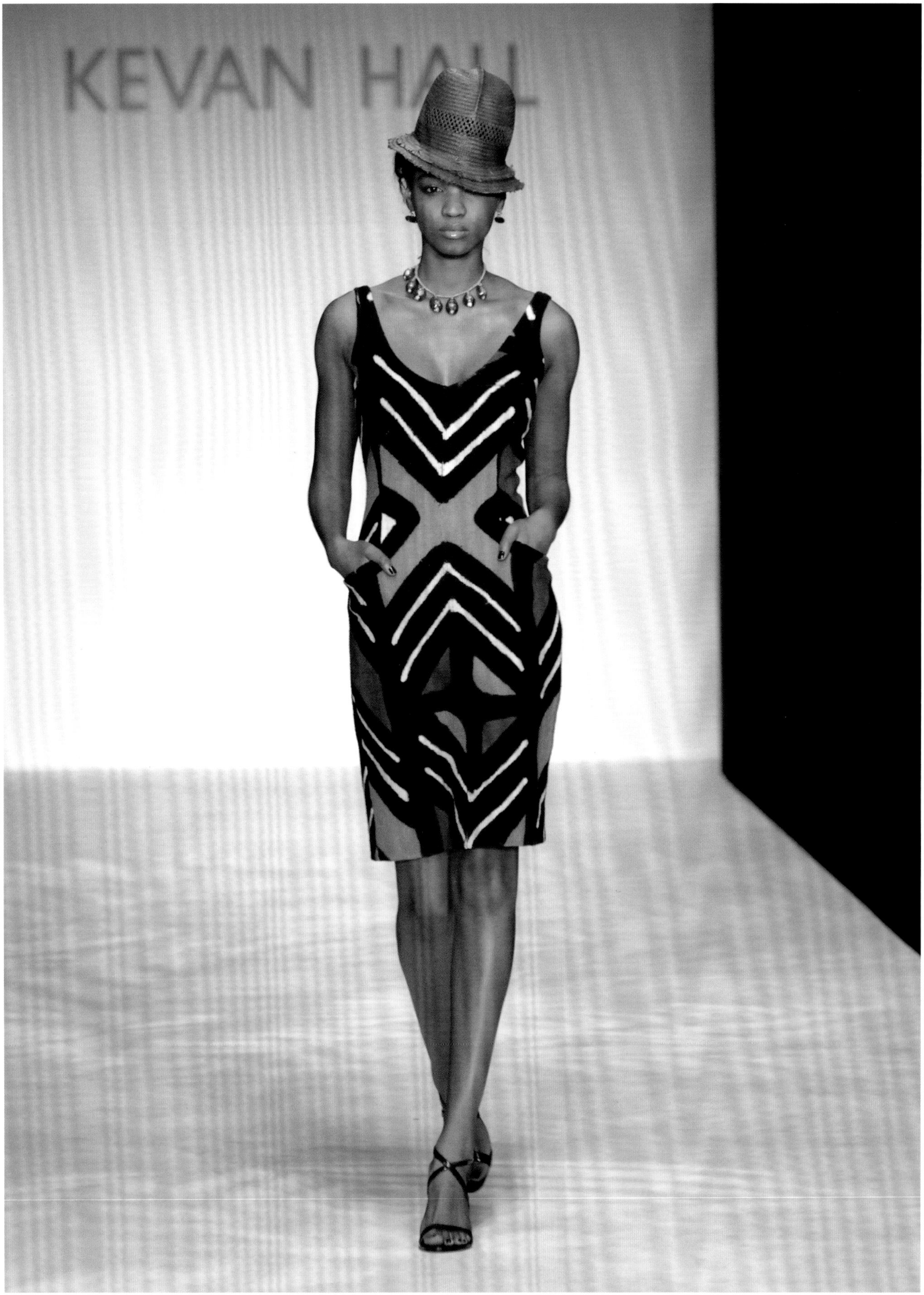
KEVAN HALL

RIGHT A look from Gwen Stefani's L.A.M.B. collection.

chapter nine

MANOLOGY

"I've got soul and I'm superbad," sang James Brown. The man with the perpetually laid-down hair spoke for himself and plenty of others when he made that declaration.

The fashion promenade would be a dry place without the soul and attention to detail that Black men bring to their appearance. There's plenty of room for authentic personal expression from many quarters, and that's a great thing. From hip hop's dookie chains, to gay life's voguing, to the sports world's baggy shorts, they've lit the matches that ignited a plethora of trends.

Pushing barriers with their style, Black men have expanded our views of masculinity. Bling in one ear or both is not especially unusual among Black men. A long line of flamboyant musicians from Little Richard to Jimi Hendrix and the late His Purpleness himself, Prince, stretched manhood's parameters to include frilly shirts, makeup, and high-heeled shoes. You may not be able to get a latte on every street corner in African-American communities, but you can find an excellent barber or braider. YouTube tells the hair story with videos highlighting hairstyles that anyone can copy: Footballer Odell Beckham Jr.'s blonde and black twists, Lil Wayne's locks, and Dwyane Wade's Caesar. Then there are the parts and patterns skillfully carved into their scalps. Yul Brynner and Telly Savalas made us hip to the fact that bald is sexy, but Michael Jordan made it popular and cool.

Back in the day, boys wanted to "be like Mike" on the court. But off-court they wanted to be like A.I. Allen "The Answer" Iverson swept in a new way to look with

OPPOSITE Singer-songwriter, rapper, record producer, film producer, and entrepreneur Pharrell Williams.

his African cornrows and enough tattoos to fill a season of A&E's *Inked*. For a while his jersey was the NBA's bestseller, outstripping champion Jordan's jersey.

The realm of sports has its own ethos. Lately, it's birthed a new generation of *GQ* profilers, both literally and figuratively. In the last decade, a bunch of athletes have spiced up *GQ* covers. Players like Russell Westbrook, Dwyane Wade, and Odell Beckham Jr. possess a penchant for decking themselves out. They've flipped the switch on high fashion by wearing the latest runway trends and designer labels and taking fashion risks. Men everywhere can relate.

In music, reggae and rap have combined to produce a robust ever-evolving cultural machine dating back to the Sixties. The rude boys, or rudies, of Kingston, Jamaica, and Derby, England, brought their toasts and their swagger to the Bronx and Brooklyn. It wasn't long before they planted the seeds for rap music and hip hop style in the Bronx.

Total assimilation was initially rare among Jamaicans in New York. As transplants, on the one hand they clung to their old ways, but on the other they absorbed the mores of their new country—a mix that gave rise to seminal figures in hip hop with deep and extant roots in Jamaica, including DJ Kool Herc (birth name Clive Campbell), Notorious B.I.G., Sandra Denton (Pepa of Salt-N-Pepa), and Busta Rhymes, to name a few of the most influential.

The impact of Black men like Marcus Garvey, Malcolm X, and Bob Marley, who left a towering legacy that included popularizing Rastafarian colors and making wearing dreads acceptable, is felt as strongly today as ever among millennials and other youth.

Style is moving away from baggy jeans hung low to show off underwear and butt cleavage. The sharp edge of menswear today is the pulled-together, formal look of a man about his business. This includes button-down shirts, jackets, tuxedos, and bow ties for day and evening. Hair is slowly coming back, especially among men under forty. There are two alternatives—a little bit of a buzz cut brushed down, or a lot of hair, grown out into a textured Afro. And guys are back to wearing do-rags at home, where they belonged all along. ∎

OPPOSITE The suave style of Terrence Howard, star of the television series *Empire*.

FOLLOWING SPREAD LEFT NFL player Odell Beckham Jr. backstage at the Nickelodeon Kids' Choice Sports Awards, 2017. The football field and YouTube videos are his stage where he's sparked a torrid following with his swagger and hairstyles.

FOLLOWING SPREAD RIGHT The hair and what to comb it with: Musician, DJ, writer, and record producer Questlove.

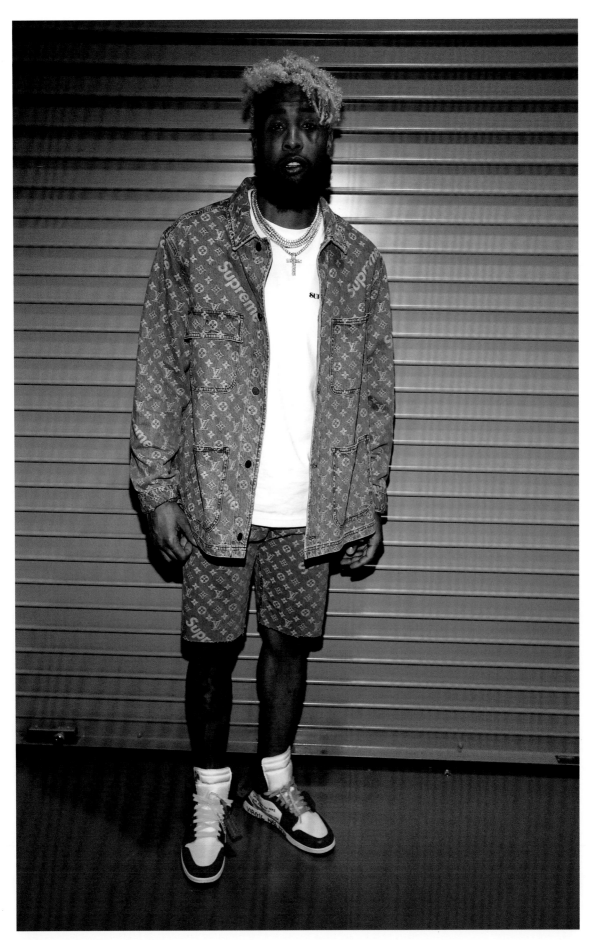

PREVIOUS SPREAD LEFT Musician Jimi Hendrix influenced many with his eclectic style, ca. late 1960s, dressing often in frilly blouses and other styles considered overtly feminine at the time.

PREVIOUS SPREAD RIGHT Black men are comfortable wearing large necklaces, earrings, rings, and other traditionally feminine accessories.

LEFT Quincy Jones, ca. 1970.

□PP□SITE The Chambers Brothers with Grace Jones, ca. 1970s.

□B□VE Mark Wahlberg when he was known as the rap artist Marky Mark, 1991. Through his music and Calvin Klein ads, he helped bring Black male rap swagger to a white youth audience.

LEFT The African-American owned and operated boutique New Breed in New York City, 1968. The shop opened in 1967 and introduced the dashiki and other African-influenced styles to America.

ABOVE Former NBA player Allen Iverson in 1999. His elaborate braids, earrings, and tattoos helped revolutionize NBA style. His jersey became the number one seller, and his Reebok "The Answer" sneakers were bestsellers.

OPPOSITE Dashikis and afros, popular in the 1960s and 1970s, are seen here on Wimbledon champion Arthur Ashe.

OPPOSITE Kanye West in a preppy designer look. His influence on style is immeasurable.

HOW TO WEAR

OPPOSITE A vest of hand-painted mud cloth, or bogolanfini, on director and producer Spike Lee, ca. 1980s. Mud cloth is a cotton cloth from Mali that is traditionally dyed with fermented mud in geometric patterns, a process that dates back to the twelfth century. Lee and Jeffrey Tweedy, formerly of Ralph Lauren, opened a path for entertainers like Puff Daddy and Jay-Z to start their own fashion labels.

OPPOSITE Jay-Z wearing a beanie from his Rocawear collection. He made the Yankee baseball cap a must-wear.

FOLLOWING SPREAD Dapper boys in the South Side of Chicago, ca. 1938.

RIGHT A still from the video for DJ Khaled's "I Got the Keys," featuring Future and Jay-Z. From left: Future, Jay-Z, DJ Khaled. The torchbearers of hip hop style have evolved to a more formal glamour.

ABOVE Slim Jxmmi (left) and Swae Lee, next-generation solo artists and brothers comprising the duo Rae Sremmurd, onstage in 2017. Their multiple tattoos, simple t-shirts, skinny dropped pants, natural hair, gold rings, and chains epitomize trends of today.

OPPOSITE Bob Marley performing onstage, 1978.

OPPOSITE Renaissance man Quade Moore mashes together skater, hip hop, and reggae style with the game-changing sneaker.

chapter ten

AMERICAN CLASSICS

Some of my favorite classics are people. Michelle Obama is a classic. Naomi Campbell is a classic. Lauryn Hill is a classic. Diahann Carroll is a classic. Billie Holiday is a classic. Muhammad Ali. A look or an accessory can be a classic, too. Kente-cloth and Holland-cloth prints are classic. The Afro is classic. The baggy jean. Hip hop with its distinctive XXL sizing, casual style, gold chains, and big earrings are classic at this point. Drake isn't classic (yet)—he's just dope. Iman's a classic. Ruby Dee, a classic.

An instant classic is oxymoronic. A classic takes time, like a good bouillabaisse. It has to simmer and sit and be tasted along the way.

When you think of a classic, what comes to mind? It might be a strand of pearls, Scottish plaids, ballet flats, or a beehive hairdo. But would you think of a dookie chain? Thinking solely in Eurocentric terms narrows perspective and limits the recognition of Black classics. From Afrocentric style come classics like kohl-rimmed eyes, exquisitely created kente cloth, dashikis, baggy jeans, djellabahs, and leopard-print anything.

A classic is part of the lexicon. It gets under the skin and becomes representative of a culture and history. A classic is cool. An American classic is something or someone we Americans are proud of and who represents the people we want to believe we are. Another kind of classic is influential. It changes things outwardly or changes people inwardly in a meaningful way. Consider the adoption of the Afro

OPPOSITE Upswept hair and a peacoat, an American classic, on model Gaye McDonald, 2007.

or the breakthrough of Naomi Campbell in fashion, her impact flowing beyond the runway to establish a feeling of pride and inspiration in Black girls everywhere.

Why is this important? Because elements of African-American style are so in, and so much a part of our lives today. Touchstones of African-American style are deeply imbedded in the broader style language of the United States no matter the color of your skin. You may not think Black style when you eyeball classics like a pair of gold hoop earrings or you slip on your sneakers for a day at the office, but that's reality. In 2017, American rapper French Montana, born in Morocco, and singer Swae Lee, born in America, jumped on a plane and flew to Kampala, Uganda, to shoot a video for their song "Unforgettable," available via the internet. The world isn't getting bigger; it's getting smaller. We can all expect to live in a future where access to fashion from Senegal to Serbia is virtually instantaneous, where the influence of cultures in places like Nigeria and India, with their growing wealth and aspiration, push the boundaries of fashion as we know it. Follow the money and the music for clues to where Afro style will go next. Meanwhile, the past stands as a monument to the richness of the record of queens and kings of style. ∎

OPPOSITE First Lady Michelle Obama, who brought prestige to American designers, in a dress by Detroit native and African American Tracy Reese.

OPPOSITE Actors Sidney Poitier and Diahann Carroll in the film *Paris Blues*, 1961, represented an American ideal of class and "good taste."

ABOVE Dancer, choreographer, and former artistic director of Alvin Ailey American Dance Theater Judith Jamison helped lay the foundation that paved the way for Misty Copeland and other dancers of color.

ABOVE The baby afro became an American classic as worn in the late Eighties by model Roshumba Williams.

ABOVE Actor and activist Ruby Dee was still slaying when she was nominated for an Academy Award in 2008 for her role in *American Gangster*. She was 86.

OPPOSITE Iman in the 1980s. Her beauty, elegance, and grace have slayed runways and magazine covers for decades.

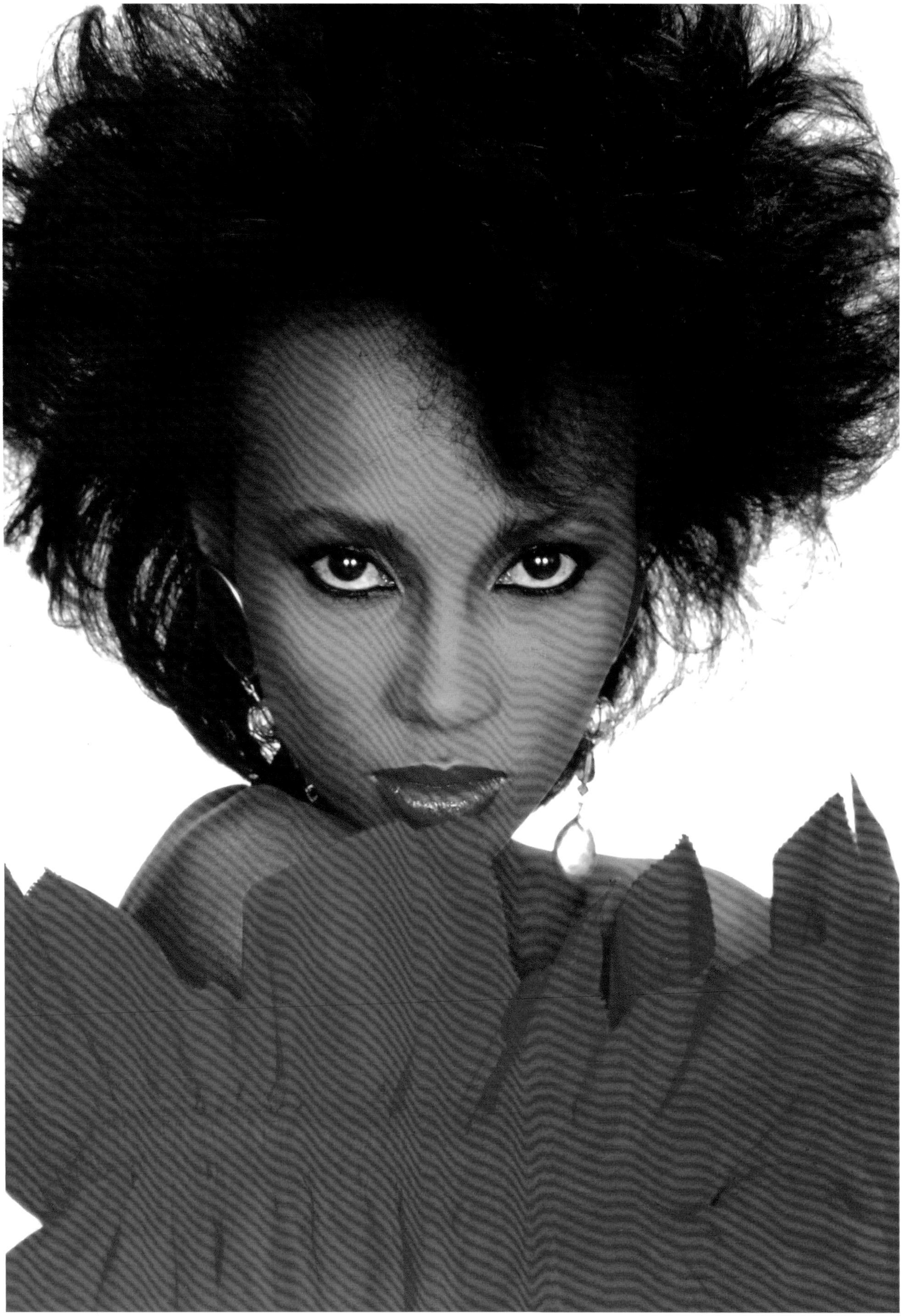

OPPOSITE Perhaps one of the best-known Americans in the world, Oprah Winfrey has been large, small, and everything in between, but she has proven many times over that size doesn't matter.

ABOVE When the Williams sisters burst onto the scene in the Nineties, their beaded braids were as much a topic of conversation as their brilliant play. Here, Serena Williams celebrates a point against Martina Hingis in the US Open, 1999.

OPPOSITE Forerunner of today's glama-track queens, gold medalist Florence Griffith Joyner took America to glory in the 1988 Seoul Olympic Games. Flo Jo is the fastest woman of all time (her records set in 1988 still stand).

OPPOSITE From left: Sandra Denton, Deidra Roper, and Cheryl James of Salt-N-Pepa helped bring to prominence this look that defined a generation.

ACKNOWLEDGMENTS

uccess has many mothers and fathers, it is said. Several people helped this book along its trajectory from composing it to getting it into your hands.

A big thank you to Marc Beckman and Nancy Chanin of DMA United, the rock stars who saw the vision. Nancy has better hair and Marc has better sneakers.

I was excited to join the Rizzoli family. I knew they would do the book justice. Thank you to editors Andrea Danese and Caitlin Leffel for their attention to detail and their help in polishing a diamond in the rough. I am grateful to Charles Miers, Rizzoli's publisher, for believing in the importance of the book.

Thank you to creative consultant Darlene Gillard Jones, who gave generous, invaluable feedback and lent her eye for fashion, photography, and African-American style.

There are startlingly few carefully crafted photographs that capture the style and panache of Black people. Graphic designer Abdullah Hassan, and photographer/filmmaker Stephen Small-Warner, who helped with early research, both provided important assistance in unearthing and assembling these evocative images.

We're all seemingly photographers today. But those who bring a special skill and passion to this visual art are as precious as unworn Air Jordan 12 Flu Game sneakers.

Anthony Barboza has shot some of the most important style moments and influencers over the last five decades with love and dedication. Itaysha Jordan's rising star is dazzling. Marc Baptiste has ascended to a level of status few Black photographers have attained, shooting top fashion and lifestyle editorials for magazines and advertising, as well as his personal projects celebrating his native Haiti. I've been privileged to work with Gilles Bensimon, one of the most important lensmen of the last three decades both here and in Europe. The talent and graciousness of Hosea Johnson, Daniela Federici, and Dan and Corina Lecca, who were the go-to photographers for the industry for many a show when we worked together for the *New York Times*, are deeply appreciated.

Thank you J. Dot and Benjamin Turbinton, IV. I am indebted to your unstinting professionalism and support.

I enjoyed finding inspiration and knowledge through books by fellow authors who've shined a light on this subject. Deborah Willis is a photographer, educator, and treasure, and she is the author of *Posing Beauty: African-American Images from the 1890s to the Present*, among other books. In addition, I was inspired by the work of professor and author Carol Tulloch in the book *Black Style* and that of my friends Duane Thomas and Lloyd Boston, who have each authored beautiful books on Black men's style. Teri Agins, author of *Hijacking The Runway: How Celebrities Are Stealing the Spotlight from Fashion Designers*, came through with her no-nonsense yet nurturing voice. During late nights and long, frantic days when I sometimes lost my way, I was able to take one or the other of these books off my shelf or coffee table and find sustenance.

Finally, I am grateful to my family, who regularly checked in, encouraged me, and offered practical assistance: I love you much. ∎

PHOTO CREDITS

OPPOSITE South African singers in Dutch cloth turbans and dresses. Face painting is a rich African legacy that is used to establish community identity; as a ritual to honor social accomplishment, social status, and spiritual connection; and as beautification for men and women.

PAGE 2 Naomi Campbell

PAGE 4 NBA player and style maven
Russell Westbrook marks a transition of
elite athletes into high fashion.

First published in the United States of America in 2018
By Rizzoli International Publications, Inc.
300 Park Avenue South
New York, NY 10010
www.rizzoliusa.com

Designed by Sarah Gifford

2018 2019 2020 2021 / 10 9 8 7 6 5 4 3 2 1

Distributed in the U.S. trade by Random House, New York

Printed in China

ISBN-13: 978-0-8478-6138-5

Library of Congress Control Number: 2017957332